2020

Veritas Mountain

1|2023

Veritas Mountain

ONE MAN'S CONTINUED JOURNEY WITH THE LORD

THIRD EDITION

Ryan Young

VERITAS MOUNTAIN
ONE MAN'S CONTINUED JOURNEY WITH THE LORD

iUniverse books may be ordered through booksellers or by contacting:

iUniverse
1663 Liberty Drive
Bloomington, IN 47403
www.iuniverse.com
1-800-Authors (1-800-288-4677)

ISBN: 978-1-6632-0290-1 (sc)
ISBN: 978-1-6632-0291-8 (e)

Print information available on the last page.

iUniverse rev. date: 06/16/2020

Contents

Dedication

This Book is dedicated:

- To my parents for forming me in the Truth.
- To my wife for keeping me in the Truth.
- To my children: What is provided in this book is the most important message I can give you as your father: I love you all. I will see you at the finish line....

Prologue

Fire, passion, grace, gratitude, purpose, identity, peace, joy.... God has been so good to me! Imagine if you had a vaccination that cures death and furthermore, would offer the recipient a life-long experience of peace and joy, regardless of worldly circumstance. All that is needed to receive this vaccination is to be humble and destroy personal EGO and pride. Sounds easy... If you can imagine the above, you understand why I am writing this book.

I am not a writer. I got "B's" in high school English and considering that I majored in biology, took little-to-no English classes in college. Writing this book is an exercise of obedience for me and an exercise on your end to deal with some pretty poor grammar. I have ADHD, not treated medically, and am surrounded by 8 children, 3 of which are under the age of 4. With kids hanging from my arms and legs and back, in between feedings, settling sibling disputes, answering the house phone, diaper changing, making dinner, going to my full - time job, and spending time with my wife and kids.... Did I mention I have ADHD? The fact that this book exists in the midst of all of that mayhem of life is a miracle, considering the rare 15 minutes in a row with which I have to write down a thought. Anything of use coming out of this tornado of my mind and life will hopefully be helpful to you on your journey.

There are no accidents. Your journey has brought you to this page, at this moment to learn something. Not everything in this book will be easy to read, much of which may strike to the depth of your heart. Do you have the courage to "Know Thy-Self?" A lot of people in our time do not have that courage. Any challenge to ingrained thoughts may cause some to run out of the room in the midst of a discussion like their hair is on fire with gross anxiety. That is why there was a movement to develop "Safe Spaces" for thought at college campuses; To have somewhere to run when one's thought process is challenged. This avoidance of conflict of thought has ultimately developed weak and close-minded, delicate people.

Truth can and must handle challenge; otherwise, by definition, it is not the Truth! If one exists in the Truth, why would they ever be anxious? If hearing another point of view causes anxiety, by definition, *that* is the time to stay and learn more. The Truth...Love, as St. Paul says, ...takes no offense. If in reading this book, you are pushed into discomfort, it is a good exercise to challenge your thought and belief. We find *rest* in the Truth!

I am a reader and talk to a lot of people, challenging my thought process and belief always. I yearn and hunger for the Truth. I have seen and experienced firsthand a lot of what the world offers. I have learned a lot. Although I have felt like I have lived many lives, and have a ton of mileage, I still enjoy learning. Half the time in this perpetual distraction of life as noted above, I forget what I was saying and return to writing this book days, if not weeks later. I then re-read the section and chuckle in gratitude to God for letting such thoughts reach paper. Hopefully, in writing this book, I can learn and grow in the process with you.

If you want to understand me, realize that although I don't know you, I love you....

Foreword

It is with tremendous honor that I take the opportunity to comment on the content of this book and the amazing man behind its words. Having known Ryan since the tender age of 18, I have had the pleasure of being by his side throughout his evolution into the man of God he is today. He is, among other things, a loving and steadfast husband, father and son, an evangelist, and a seeker of Truth and Justice. He has conquered many obstacles to become those things over the years and has been a hero to me with his unwavering devotion to discerning the Will of God in his life.

If there is one impression many people have after a conversation with Ryan, it is that he is passionate and dedicated to not only what he currently believes, but also to the search for something more: Truth. I have witnessed him spending his adult life in the pursuit of Wisdom and Justice, attempting to learn more about the God with whom he wants to spend the rest of his eternal life. His spiritual journey has consisted mainly of seeking, recognizing, internalizing, defending, teaching, and sharing little morsels of truth he has gathered throughout the years.

Collecting the tidbits set forth in this book about various subjects has been an adventure of sorts. Ryan would not consider himself a scholar, but he has been open to hearing and absorbing the advice and insights of all of those around him, likeminded or not. I have been with my husband for the formation of many of the thoughts in this book, whether derived from meditation, dinners with friends and family, consults with his patients, books, the Bible, the Catholic Catechism, or even movies. I can attest to the earnest process by which Ryan carefully and prayerfully separates out the truth in what he hears and reads. This book was not meant to be a textbook, but Ryan has painstakingly tried to ascertain the validity of his opinions prior to including them. If there are items that do not conform to the truths held within Catholic teaching, I can assure you that it is truly unintentional on his part.

Along the way, many of our friends and relatives have been instrumental in not only shaping and refining Ryan's thoughts, but also encouraging the propagation of these teachings through inviting him to speak to a large group or supporting him in the formation of a youth camp. Ryan has formed stores of appropriate stories and words of wisdom for various daily struggles and has been bold enough to share these when he encountered someone in need of comfort or help finding God. The process began many, many years ago of starting to record the stories mainly so he would not forget them. This book has now evolved into a record of these insights; however, it began as simply a way for a loving father to share his journey with the Lord for the sake of his children. As a father, he wants only that his children have eternal life with God. His secondary desire is for his children to know him, love him and want to be with him forever, much as Ryan's only life's goal has become to know God, love God, and be with Him forever in Heaven.

Ryan firmly believes that we are in a war for souls. In writing this book, he hopes to arm his children with a shield of self-awareness and a sword of Truth. I could not be more proud of the man Ryan has become, and in many ways has always been. He is a true inspiration to me, our family, our friends and our community and I am not ashamed to say that I consider myself the luckiest woman alive to be at his side in his journey to Christ. Enjoy this book as I have enjoyed immensely the many nights we have labored together over the formation of its contents.

Forever in Christ,
Elizabeth Young

The Autopsy

It was a gray, colorless, December day in Long Island when my daughter Trinity and I drove into this highly outdated governmental building complex. I have 8 kids and we cannot afford to have our kids go to college and "find themselves," changing majors multiple times while extending the very expensive college experience. We also don't want to have them get a degree, get to their first job, and then hate their work for the rest of their life when in reality their job is not as interesting as was anticipated. Therefore, before picking a college major, we require our kids to follow somebody in the field of interest for a day or two in order to determine if that is what they really want to do.

My challenge with Trinity is that she is brilliant. With brilliance comes almost too many options. One day she wants to be an actress. The next day she wants to be a fighter pilot. The next a writer. The next a teacher.... You get my point.

After watching CSI shows on TV, she was interested in crime-scene investigation. I knew she would even consider being a medical examiner. She would be surrounded by death all day—from children, the elderly and everybody in between. She would examine death from finding bodies weeks to months after they passed, to car accidents, to drug overdoses, to child abuse, to burn victims, to every horrid situation involving death. She would be the person talking to families and bringing those who are grieving the answer to their questions. I made a few calls and a Physician Assistant in the CSI field invited us to observe the morning autopsies.

We entered the outdated building with a 70's décor including lime green fading floor tiling and a smell like a nursing home. The building was staffed by an assortment of highly pierced and tattooed, heavy coffee drinking, cigarette smoking crew of various ages. We were invited back

1

to the cooler where four men were naked and completely exposed on steel gurneys in the hallway. I glanced into the cooler to the right and saw at least 30 more bodies awaiting their turn. Looking at them and knowing nothing, one could not tell if they were millionaires or homeless. If they were loved or hated. If they were saints or criminals. If they were brilliant, funny, or compassionate. Looking at these 4 naked dead men, I realized pretty quickly that we will all end up like this one day, leaving the earth naked as the day we were born. Our bodies will not last forever. It was like a black and white dream.

As we entered the lab, they allowed Trinity and I to stand at the table at the base of the autopsy. The medical examiner was a fairly young, black woman who entered the room and had a look of intensity and focus. She read out the gentlemen's name, Hernando, and stated the cause of death; Suicide. This man hung himself 8 hours earlier. She then made her "Y" incision over his chest and started to rapidly remove all of his organs, placing them directly in front of me and Trinity.

This was not the first time I have seen and worked with death. As a Physician Assistant myself, we worked with cadavers throughout my education. The difference between cadavers and Hernando's body is that cadavers are dry. All fluids are removed and replaced with preservatives which also have a distinct smell. These organs however were juicy and fresh and basically odorless. They were perfect. As the lungs were placed in front of us, followed by the heart, followed by the kidneys, followed by the liver and spleen, one could only stand in awe witnessing the perfection of our body, all parts having a distinct and critical role in our survival, working perfectly in unison.

Right now as you read this book, your heart beats, your body temperature is roughly 98.6 degrees (not 70 or 130), you're digesting your last meal to obtain energy from the food while separating it from waste, you have balance, hearing, smell, sight, taste and touch with millions of receptors taking in input, with hormones and feedback systems governing the functions of most organs. You have trillions of cells working in unison. If you get a cut on your hand, these cells identify the injury, then repair the injury level by level until it heals. One also does not develop an ear growing from their hand when it heals. We have the ability to watch this miracle, yes miracle, in action. Science knows *that* these biological processes occur and have even named them, but nobody knows *how* these processes actually work.

What has always amused me with atheists is their belief that this life that we observe all around us *comes from a rock.* Mind you, that they will state that they will believe nothing that they cannot see, feel, prove, re-prove, and so forth. Right now, taught in every public school throughout the planet, we are taught that after the big bang which shot rocks all over the universe (actually presented by a Catholic priest), that from the rock of the earth, having absolutely nothing to do with evolution, life just began.

Looking at those perfect organs sitting 1 foot from us, I chuckled at the absurdity of that thought. Afterall, *where is the rock*? Where has this been proven? How does a rock create a single cell? The body is a miracle. All life, from the trees to the animals, and everything else alive in nature is a miracle. Even the forces it takes to sustain life are miraculous. So many factors must be perfect for us to live to our natural death. So many factors... It must be some rock!!

Despite witnessing the biological miracle of our body 2 feet from us, it was blatantly obvious to me as I stood in front of Hernando's miraculous body that Hernando *was not there!* As amazing as our hearts are, we can have that thumping organ of a heart beating for 100 years but that is still not what makes us great. We have consciousness! We have the ability to think, love, create, destroy, forgive, communicate, dream, and choose. We have that breath of God in all of us, that extra part, that energy, that eternal soul. Our bodies only cart this soul around. **What rock creates consciousness?**

I have a severe handicap with names. It has caused me strife throughout my life because everybody knows me. After seeing over 100,000 patients in my region, singing in my church for 18 years, leading thousands to the Truth every summer, being on America's Most Wanted... just waking you back up.... I cannot go anywhere without being stopped and people asking me about the family and so forth. I detest not remembering most people's names...

I remember Hernando's name. I remember it because he had this miracle of life, and threw it away. He most certainly encountered hardship and had no hope, no point, no identity, and found no purpose. The bodies to be examined after his were two people who overdosed on drugs and one person who died of natural causes. If Hernando had only known the Truth and lived in Reality, he could have experienced peace and joy in all of life's curveballs...

I wish I would have met him when he was still here. I pray that I do not take for granted those I encounter daily. I pray for him from time to time. I do not believe in accidents. His death further woke me up to the Reality of Truth. I hope to see him when my time is up to thank him for that. Once again, in experiencing the miracle of life itself in this way, I had to again ask myself, "Why are we here?" What is the Meaning to Life?

The Meaning of Life

Tick, tock, tick, tock, tick, tock… time. I started to think a lot about time when I was just beginning high school. Time was passing and passing by quickly and I didn't have a point to my life. I found myself locked in a routine. Mine consisted of waking up before sunrise to the obnoxious beeping of my alarm clock, showering in cold water (I was always competing for hot water with my six sisters), eating nearly the same thing every day for breakfast and lunch, waiting for the bus, going to class, working after school, watching TV, talking to friends and then repeating the same pointless routine, day after day after day. Why, I finally asked? Was there anything that I was doing with my time on a daily basis that was actually going to last? Is there more to life than whether the Jets win on Sunday or who in Hollywood is cheating with whom? The interests of the world seemed so shallow. At the end of my days I knew I would die. I knew that we all have a 100% mortality rate, the question is simply when. Why bother with the effort of life if it would all end anyway? Why spend all my time doing what the world expected me to do? Without a reason to my life, I was living a life without peace and joy. My life felt so shallow, so empty.

Before having purpose and meaning to my life, I had moments of "happiness." I would feel happy when I felt "full" emotionally, physically, and mentally. The problem with my life and my actions at that time was that the happiness that I experienced was fleeting and brief. I was always looking for the next big fix, which might be experienced with one more vacation, one more material good, one more girlfriend, one more achieved earthly success. I was never able to sustain that feeling of "happiness" and would always return to that inner void of emptiness. What I really sought was meaning and purpose to my life.

I call it the "Superbowl syndrome." Imagine a professional athlete practicing football his whole life and finally making the NFL. After years in the NFL, he finally makes it on a team that wins a lot of games. He gives it his all throughout the season, diving and fighting for the ball. He finally makes it to the Superbowl and his team wins. He experiences absolute jubilation and 'happiness' for about five minutes. He then asks himself, "now what?" I had to reevaluate. What were my 'Superbowl' ambitions? Were my objectives *lasting* objectives?

When I was in high school, I would set a goal for myself like getting an 'A' on a test or win a championship in sports. I would study or play hard and yes, at times I would actually stumble upon the 'A' or trophy I sought (even a blind squirrel finds a nut every once in a while). My motivation at the time was completely about self. I was getting the 'A' to receive praise from my parents and peers, as well as to make a lot of money one day. I worked on earning trophies so I could impress the young ladies at school. I was studying for accolades so at some point, I could garner respect. At the time, **nearly every motivation of every act I did was to build self.** Every act I did was to earn gains in the trio of earthly sex, money, and power. I wanted control.

Since then I have observed thousands of people, of all ages, wandering through life the way I did in high school. I used to work in New York City and commute every day on the train. People in suits would be holding the same kind of coffee in one hand, with the same newspaper in the other, and would know the exact spot where the train door would open once it would finally arrive. They would enter the train and sit in the same seat they always used. It was robotic. It is not that I perceive a routine as evil. However, there has to be more to life than this superficiality.

I was able to avoid the fate of the emptiness of routine because I stopped to ask the question: Why? Why are we here? What is the point of life? I believe all humans have asked these questions consciously or subconsciously at some time during their life. There seems to be some kind of magnet in our human chemistry that draws us to seek the Truth in this regard.

As discussed regarding the autopsy, I don't believe we came from a rock. I believe we were created by God in His image and likeness. Professionally, I am a scientist of sorts. I think the world mistakenly perceives that science is the attempt to disprove the existence of God. I believe that **science is the study *of* the creation of God.** As I look at science in that light, it completely enhances my knowledge of God and Creation and consequently, my relationship with God deepens even further. I am able to marvel at His grandeur in space, the environment, and our bodies.

I am not alone in this view of science. Many scientists initially set out to disprove God and then discovered in their scientific pursuit that the mathematical possibility of us existing without Him is essentially impossible. I would argue that an Atheist requires far more "faith" in the impossible than one who acknowledges the existence of God.

What about evolution? I don't think it matters. Evolution does not disprove God. You would still need God to create something before that something could evolve. You would still need order and oversight to keep life in existence. If God created the universe and that universe evolved with God's oversight, who cares whether or not evolution exists? The Truth is *He created us either way.*

After we conclude that God must exist, I still questioned, "why me?" Why did He create me? Why give us this life? In my observation of people, I came to a startling realization: we have been *given* everything that identifies us. We were born into our bodies, our looks, talents, family, country, wealth, station, everything. We had no control over any of these things at birth. We have limited control over these realities even as we get older. Whether you were born predisposed to being rich, poor, fat, skinny, ugly, gorgeous, psychologically imbalanced, intelligent, or any combination thereof, we all have only one thing in common from birth: *our free will.* **The only common attribute of all human beings is the ability to choose, moment to moment, what we are going to do with the station, talents, looks, intelligence, wealth, and so forth that we have been given.** This Truth brought me to understand the meaning of life. **THE MEANING OF LIFE IS TO *CHOOSE* ETERNITY WITH GOD!!!!**

We have been given this split second, this blink of eternity's eye, to make a choice. Again, I found that if I believe in God and understand that my only possession is my free will, what else could this life be for? If you loved someone, would you force them to be with you for eternity? If you were a parent and you shackled your kids to the floor of your basement for eternity stating "I will force you to be with me and you must love me," *is that love?* **Can there be love or relationship without the freedom to choose it?** If God created us without choice and chained us to Heaven's wall, could you call that love or would it become slavery?

In order for us to have the capacity to love, we must have the choice of *not* loving. Love itself cannot exist without a free-will. Once I understood that my purpose in life is this decision to choose relationship with Him, to choose Love, everything came into focus. Now there is a reason for my existence. Now there is a purpose to every breath I take on a daily basis. Now there is a reason for every action and decision I make. Life has become a lot more meaningful.

Once I found that Heaven is my objective, my entire "priority list of life" changed. **What is more important than Heaven?!!** My relationship with God and His mission for me now takes precedence over all my former "worldly" goals. If I am the most "successful" individual in every earthly way, including family, money, power, education, and earthly influence, and then die and have not chosen relationship with God, my entire life has been an utter waste. If I do not choose Heaven, I truly would have lived a meaningless life and would have wasted the very point of my existence. Without choosing relationship with God, I could not be further from the Truth and Reality of my creation, in fact I would have just wasted the very essence of everything I was built to be. I would be no more valuable than the dust of the earth.

Now, the priority of my life is to strive for eternity with God. That priority influences every decision I make. This influenced which college I attended, who I decided to marry, what major I chose in college, my political affiliation, my identity... everything. There is no decision on earth that would warrant ignoring the objective of Heaven and avoiding my relationship with God.

In understanding the meaning of life, I now experience joy. The difference between the happiness I would formerly experience in reaching my worldly goals, and joy, is that *joy lasts*. I perpetually feel good at my emotional baseline. I feel other emotions like sadness, anger, jealousy, happiness, ambition, inadequacy, and so forth, but at my baseline, I always return to joy. I have peace. I know where I came from and where I am going. My daily routine now has purpose. I am no longer just "going through the motions of life." The journey of Life has become so much easier that I feel like I am walking downhill.

Not everyone in the world has *worldly* freedom. Some people are born into tyranny. However, with a free will, we can all have *spiritual* freedom. We have the freedom to use our free will in every situation, good or bad, and we have the freedom to use our free will to choose relationship with God... or not.

Please don't think I am saying that if you understand the meaning of your life, you will not suffer. The truth is quite different. The truth is that even while suffering—if you and I understand that in every moment of every day we have an opportunity to choose God—we can be joyful in that suffering. This was shown by the first Christian martyrs as they were burned alive or fed to lions in the Colosseum. They were joyful and singing at their deaths. The point is this: **if you constantly choose relationship with God, in good situations and bad, you will have peace and joy at all times**. Lord, thank you for giving me purpose. Lord, thank you for drawing me to you. It was when I realized the true meaning of my life that my adventure with the Lord began.

Choice

It is 8:23am in Baghdad, Iraq. This day, my mission and the fulfillment and culmination of my life will reach its apex. Thirteen minutes left. I am excited and anxious at this moment. I can feel sweat dripping down my back and covering my forehead under my turban. I don't know if I am sweating because of the stifling heat? I don't know if it's from the weight of the fiery deliverance buckled around my waist? I don't know if it's from fear? I am so petrified that I can taste bile in my mouth. Regardless, the harem that awaits me in heaven as promised by my earthly spiritual teacher, Mohammed Al Jahiff, is worth a bit of sweat and fear. I finally received the call by cell phone last night. I have prepared my whole life for this moment at my madrasa and I will not fail. These American infidels and Iraqi police, these traitors of Islam are about to know Allah's wrath! I feel honored that I can play a role in this holy Jihad. Here comes my target. These guys have no idea about what is about to hit them. It is time to reach for the trigger. Three, two, one, Praise ALLAH!..... BOOM!

This teenage Islamic male just died believing he was choosing God. Was he? How do we know? What is our standard for that perfect choice? Many will read that story and start a mental series of justifications for why they don't believe in "organized religion." They convince themselves to suspend the search for Truth altogether, and continue to purposely and intentionally *go out of their way* to avoid God as much as possible. They will choose to live life without meaning or purpose, choosing a finite life of emptiness and ignorance of the Truth, with rare moments of fleeting happiness, and will ignore the bigger picture of their existence. **We are meant for more than a shallow life!**

Some completely discount all the knowledge and wisdom of everybody throughout the history of the world who have asked the same questions and who have often received sound answers in Truth through reason. Those who simply dump "organized religion," instead of standing on the shoulders of theological giants, start again to "create the wheel" on their own. Is this a wise course of action? Is it wise to believe that no one else throughout the history of our planet has ever had a thought in philosophy or theology that was a pretty good idea? It would be as foolish as trying to invent a computer from scratch at this point without first looking at and taking apart computers that presently exist.

Why are questions regarding religion off limits? Why does it seem so natural to ask advice about which car to buy, what to name your child, which doctor to see about your allergies, what school to attend and which outfit to wear to a certain event, but not seek or accept advice about our spiritual health? Why does it seem taboo to openly discuss what others believe and why? In reality, most "intellectuals" who avoid God are just spiritually insecure or theologically lazy or they just do not want to acknowledge the Truth that there is a God, *and it is not them.*

What is ironic about this avoidance of God is that these same intellectuals generally affirm that they believe in the concept of good and evil. They would generally acknowledge a difference between the actions and beliefs of Hitler and Mother Theresa. They generally agree that the concepts of the Ten Commandments and charity and so forth are "good acts." If one believes in good and evil, inherently they must also believe in God because otherwise "good" would not be defined by anything and there would be chaos. **Without God, there is no order. Without God, there is no Truth. Without God, there is no difference between Hitler and Mother Theresa. Without God, we are just blobs of matter passing through the universe without point. Without God,** *there is no such thing as good and evil. What do you believe?*

From time to time, I attend black tie gala's for various philanthropic purposes. A couple of years ago at a Gala for our local hospital, I happened to be sitting next to several people, including one of our local abortionists, and several others on the board of our local Planned Parenthood, who were soliciting me to support Planned Parenthood with time and money. Clearly, they had no idea that they were sitting next to an actual Knight of the Roman Catholic Church as a member of its oldest lay religious order. As I smiled and subtly felt my wife's hand grabbing my leg as a reminder of loving prudence, I remembered my first objective is to love them all. *Lasting conversion is not possible without love.* This was not the time, nor the place for meaningful conversation, or for them to know without a shadow of a doubt that I love them, or was it?

As I smiled and nodded politely, and as our conversation continued, I was asked about our children. As I noted that we just had our 6th child at the time, there was a collective gasp at the table. The woman next to me hissed in disgust, "You must be Catholic." With a smile, I answered, "I sure am!" She then went on to tell me about my ignorance because of my belief in God. She also shared that she grew up Catholic and was "liberated" (from reality). I sensed there was anger with God within her and she was trying to punish Him with disbelief.

As I answered her challenges to Faith, answering question by question with confidence and reason, peace and joy, interest in her through love, she became frustrated. Finally, she stated, "Without Jesus Christ, you have *nothing!*" I responded, "Without Jesus Christ, *you* have nothing."

Jesus. Here comes that name again. Over and over. Jesus Jesus Jesus. Why are we still talking about him 2000 years later? Perhaps it is because despite Christ being born amongst the poor, despite being the only child of nobody in the middle of nowhere, despite not writing down anything Himself and having only 3 years of ministry before his death, despite not having TV or newspapers or the internet 2000 years ago, we are *still* talking about Him. He was obviously worth talking about and remembering. Through his miracles and teaching and through its effect on his followers, even to their horrible death, there incarnate, was the answer to our deepest questions. **There, *in person*, was the deepest longing of our soul satisfied.** *Perhaps, it is time to listen.*

God gave us the perfect standard of Good and Evil. He gave us "the Way, the Truth, and the Life."(Jn 14:16) He gave us *Himself* as Jesus Christ. Who would be a better example of perfection than God Himself? No longer is the choice for God ambiguous. No longer is Truth some vague, gray, abstract, unattainable idea. In the Incarnation of God into the man of Jesus Christ, no longer is God some being out in space that is completely out of touch with Humanity. Through the life of Jesus Christ, Reality in Truth for the perfection of our will walked the very Earth in which we now live. He breathed the same air. In His humanity, He was tempted and suffered yet He still lived perfection, as He was God.

This Good News of the Incarnation, God becoming man, was shouted in praise from the Heavens both at the Annunciation (When the Archangel Gabriel revealed to Mary that she would bear the savior of the world) and from legions of angels at Christmas to the Shepherds "And suddenly there was a multitude of the heavenly hosts with the angel, praising God and saying: "Glory to God in the highest and on Earth peace to those on whom his favor rests."(Lk 2:13).

Why Jesus? Why not Mohammed, or John Smith, or Buddha and so forth? I ultimately had to ask myself this question, "If I were to choose from all the prophets and holy men throughout time to be my savior, my 'perfect example and choice,' who would it be?" If the meaning of life is to choose God, I have yet to find another religion where God *Himself* came to Earth to be the "Perfect Choice" and ultimately redeem mankind. Other religions have a "great prophet," but they don't claim to have God Himself as their standard.

The most basic moral standard of our country and most the world is generally, "Do unto others what you would have them do unto you." The world's basic moral standard (Natural Law) follows the teaching of Jesus, whether the world knows this or not. There is no individual throughout all of time that has more dramatically changed the world's view of morality than Jesus Christ. I would love to tell you every detail I know about His life at this moment, but I would not have enough pages in this book to do so. If you are reading this book and do not know about the life of Jesus Christ, I implore you to read the 4 Gospels in the New Testament or even watch the movie "Jesus of Nazareth,"(1977), which may be cinematically outdated, but is a solid and scripturally based movie about the life of Jesus. Once you do that, you will then have to make a decision identified accurately by C.S. Lewis in "Mere Christianity." Either Jesus is a complete lunatic because He claims to be the Son of Man (God Himself), or Jesus Christ is who He claims He is. How could He be considered a "great prophet" or "nice historical figure" if He was a lunatic and a liar? *Which do you believe?*

Evidence of Christ's divinity was demonstrated by the stories documented throughout the New Testament. His divine life was outlined before Christ's birth through prophecy and revelation throughout the entire Old Testament. It was seen at His birth as Herod was willing to kill all male children less than two years of age in Christ's hometown of Bethlehem to prevent Christ from maturing. Again, even His enemies had faith in who He was. It was seen by three foreign Kings coming to pay Him homage. This was seen through His miracles that were acknowledged by both His friends *and* His enemies. This was proven most as he rose from the dead following his crucifixion. Christ's message fulfills the longing for Truth in every human heart. Christ's divinity is confirmed when all of his apostles except John were tortured to death and martyred for their faith. For the sake of argument, if they were just making this whole thing up, why were they willing to die horrible deaths for a hoax or a lie?

If you have a general knowledge of the life of Christ and you are not sure whether He is a lunatic and a liar or that Christ is truly the Son of God, I ask you to consider performing a simple spiritual exercise. Find a large crucifix. Staring at Jesus on the cross, I want you to repeat out loud ten times, "Jesus, you are a lunatic, a liar, and a fraud. You did not die on that cross for me." In performing this exercise, it will force most to get off "the fence" and make a decision. If you can make it through that statement ten times and mean it, the rest of this book might not be very relevant to you yet because you have yet to know the basics of who Jesus is.

If you are with me up to this point and believe that God created us, gave us a free will to choose Him, and that Jesus Christ is the Truth, the Perfect Choice, then welcome to Christianity! Accepting the Bible as an authority for Truth *only then* makes sense. The entire Old Testament points to the coming of the Messiah. It is incredible that the lessons of the Old Testament and spiritual struggles of mankind thousands of years before the birth of Christ are the same battles we fight today. The Truth in Scripture stands out for this reason. Its Truth transcends time. The entire Old Testament ultimately provides only a shadow of God and His Will for us. Through the Old Testament God communicates through signs and wonders and prophets. It is only in the New Testament where the shadow of God is lifted by God Himself through becoming directly present to His people in the person of Christ Jesus. God has made it clear that if we can emulate Christ and follow His teaching, we will make the "perfect choice." We will be making the choice of Heaven as our ultimate objective.

If Christ is the Way, the Truth, and the Life, there is no further prophet needed to relay the wishes of God. Who can better offer us Truth than God Himself? That is why other religious texts, such as the Koran or the Book of Mormon that were written well after the life of Christ, are not necessary in the search for Truth. Christ didn't say "I am *mostly* the Truth and some other prophet will need to come after my time and finish the job…" As far as I know, neither those of Islam nor Mormons believe that Christ is a lunatic or a liar. The reasoning for the need of the teaching of Mohammed or John Smith is therefore unclear to me. That being said, many Muslims and Mormons, through their inherent desire to be good, whether they know it or not, *live* the life of Christ better than some Christians whose actions do not support what they supposedly believe. Who then, is making a better "choice" for God? Who then has a better relationship with God? Who then would most likely rest in His arms as would a child for eternity?

In my walk with the Lord, the awareness of these realities started to bring focus to my mission. That mission is to know Christ and to follow Christ as his disciple. The Truth sets me free of the worldly illusion to aspire for a meaningless, superficial life. In following Christ, I am free from the mental and spiritual programming of our society and culture. I am no longer deceived in the lie that sex, money, and power will bring me lasting joy. It is like tearing off the scales from my eyes and I can see the exciting Good News in the Truth – Jesus Christ! I AM FREE!! In many ways, by following Christ, I have experienced a taste of Heaven here on Earth. By acknowledging the Truth of Christ, I now have a spiritual focus and can live in the Truth with the *confidence* of knowing right from wrong, good from evil. I can be confident about the impact of my behavior. I now have a goal of perfection that I can attempt to reach. I now have lasting peace in the confidence that I am choosing Truth, thus I am choosing relationship with God, and will ultimately be in His arms for eternity in paradise. Jesus truly is the Way, the Truth, and the Life!

The Religion of Self

I recently attended a Mass in upstate New York, and noted that the church was hardly attended. Those who were present were old. The priest, who was covering numerous parishes on his own, was old. There is only one shared Mass per weekend. Other than my family, there was no one in attendance under the age of 60. There was not even an organist. For one who absolutely loves the Church, it was like standing at the bedside of a family member that you deeply love that is terminally ill from a preventable disease. There is a feeling of helplessness. There is a sense of "How did we come to this?" The Catholic Church in that region will likely not exist ten years from now. I have attended many churches throughout the Northeast and noticed similar situations. The Catholic Church, as we know it, is dying in that area of our country.

It reminds me of my college semester abroad in Europe. I went into these fantastic, immense cathedrals throughout France, Germany, Hungary, and the Czech Republic, only to find the cathedrals nearly empty for Mass. It was like walking into a cold, dark tomb. These massive buildings were corpses of the life that once lived within them. That life was the Church, the community of believers who once worshipped together in unison as one body. This Church, this community of people cared for one another and was connected to the lives of the other members of that body. This community shared in each family's high points, such as a baptism and first communion, and would also be there for a family's low points, such as providing help when needed or being present to lend support during the death of one of its members. The church was a spiritual family then in that region.

One afternoon I was talking to one of my childhood best friends. We were reflecting on the condition of the Catholic Church in today's society. I was very sad at the prospect of such goodness in our Church seemingly dying in my sight. He said something very profound. He noted that we now live in a society of individualism where the very concept of community and family is under full attack. With the family community under attack, the attack on the larger church community of the faithful would reasonably follow. In short, **the Church is ill because the family is ill. Why? Because the Church is family. The Church is relationship.**

This made a lot of sense to me. We now live in the age of "Seinfeld." I love watching that show. Occasionally, I still capture the episodes on my DVR. I find the program quite humorous. However, what disturbs me is that many of my friends and peers are actually living lives like those portrayed on that show. On the program you see four people living individual lives without a serious *commitment* to anything or anybody. They are gods unto themselves. There is never a moment when any one of them would *sacrifice* anything for anybody else. They simply live an amoral life, finding the next "fix" of happiness with their next meal, date, snapchat, or entertainment prospect. Every moment of every day, their goal is to satisfy every animalistic desire… to feel emotionally full for a few moments. Every moment of every day is used to satisfy *self*. This drive to satisfy their emotional hunger is at any cost, regardless of the damage done to themselves, others, or the community at large. In the end there is nothing but absolute emptiness and loneliness. **In the end, there is nothing but *self*.** Instead of watching this TV series as an entertaining fictional story and satire of our culture, the "Seinfeld lifestyle" has now become the cultural "norm."

Growing up, the world promoted self above all else. I spent much of my youth preparing for the day when I would finally meet my spouse; the woman I had been praying for and about for years before I actually met her. Although I did not believe in this kind of thing at the time, when I finally met her at the age of 18 at an ice cream social the second day of college, I knew my life was hers. There was a kind of recognition, like remembering a dream. I finally met my other half; my "bone of my bones and flesh of my flesh," (Gen 2:23) my Eve. It was this moment after mere seconds of conversation that I told my older brother Robert, "I have found my wife." He logically looked at me skeptically and stated, "Buddy, there are many great fish in this larger pond of college, slow down little brother."

Regardless of his advice, I simply knew. I don't know how, I just knew she was me. The first Thanksgiving of freshman year of college, I slapped down her picture on the Thanksgiving table in front of my eight brothers and sisters and parents declaring that this shall be my wife! After rolling their eyes, they asked if I was even dating her yet. I confidently exclaimed "that she had a serious boyfriend that she thought she was going to marry," but I wasn't too worried about that… We did not even start dating till the following summer. We were engaged the summer after and I proposed to marry her following our third year in college. Little did I know the kind of backlash I was about to face!

When I decided to ask my wife to marry me, I cannot tell you how many people advised me to wait until I "established myself" before I got married. In essence, I was told to live this "Religion of self," this "Religion of Individualism" before giving myself up to the *commitment* of family. In the "Religion of Self," *my* needs were to come first. If it feels good, do it. In the "Religion of self," *I* am in control. In this religion, *I* am god. *My* education, my power was to come first. *My* career and money were to come first. There was nothing more important than *my* immediate pleasure, *my* quest for sex, so I should live a life that pretends I am married while living with a girlfriend, but without the commitment. Why avoid commitment one might ask? So I can easily *leave* the day any remote sacrifice is needed of me. This is the teaching of the world! Self, self, self, self, self!!! **There is nothing more threatening to the "Religion of Self" than the giving of self in marriage! There is *absolutely* nothing more threatening to the "Religion of Self" than the *sacrificial love* involved in bearing children!!** The "Religion of Self" is why abortion is viewed as 'necessary' today. The root of every abortion is self. The "Religion of Self" is why most are choosing to delay getting marriage till their late twenties and thirties. The "Religion of Self" is why there is a 50% divorce rate. Wake up brothers and sisters! "The Religion of Self" has taken a serious foothold over our culture!

My answer to the world was that I *knew* this woman was my wife. If I still needed more education, we would experience that together. If I was to be poor, and believe me, we were really poor (the entire belongings of both of us combined fit into a sedan. We literally sat on the floor of our first apartment and used our igloo cooler as our table), at least we would be poor *together in marriage.* We could not even afford a toilet paper holder for the first 3 years of marriage. Yes, you heard me right, a $10 toilet paper holder! If we were going to be poor separately, we might as well be poor together.

My point has been and still is that I will love her in good times and bad, in sickness and in health, for richer or poorer, till death we part. That was my oath to her. That remains my oath and my covenant to her this very day. **There is nothing to say what tomorrow will bring.** What is our oath/covenant worth? Does commitment mean anything? Do we understand that there is **no such thing as love without *sacrifice*?!!** **Denial and ultimately death to self is the path of real, lasting love.** This statement is anathema to the "Religion of Self." In the "Religion of Self," one can only sacrifice and live for *self.*

The "Religion of Self" has bled into the thought process of our entire culture. Our country's national debt is one more symptom of this "Religion of Self." We used to live in a country where we worked hard in order to provide our children with a future *better* than our own. No longer. We now use more money than what exists in Medicare and Social Security, not adjusting for life expectancy or how much was originally invested into these social programs, dropping the burden of debt onto our children in order to get every 'entitlement' we can drown ourselves in today. Imagine at your parent's death, they left you a $200,000 debt that you had to pay now. That is the situation in which we are leaving our children. We are totally selfish.

Through our desire to control everything and be our own gods, the family unit and the essence of community is under attack. The fabric of our society, which is the family, is 'thread bare." The family is like an orchestra with many parts that, when working in unison, creates a symphony. If everyone in the family is living the "Religion of Self" and plays his own tune, the resulting music will sound disastrous. The family is the building block of all society. If society does not have a solid base in the family, all aspects of that society will suffer and ultimately collapse. Think about how many problems are rampant in our society today due to the lack of a strong family unit. Think about how many families no longer have a matriarch and a patriarch. The fight for control and power in our lives through the attempt to build self, is causing divorce, fornication, and selfishness to become our cultural "norm." **In this modern era of self, are we truly better off? Do more people have lasting joy in their lives?**

The Church is a family. The Church is a community. The Church is relationship. The Church is referred to as "The body of Christ."(1Cor12:12) The Church is the antithesis of the "Religion of Self!"

In the "church" of my home, my family helps keep me grounded. My precious wife Elizabeth keeps my eyes focused on the "finish line" of Heaven. How often I am tempted to live only for myself. We are back to back in the trenches of life. We gave ourselves to each other, totally and completely, in the holy sacrament of Matrimony. I have truly come to understand the statement that "two come together and make one flesh."(Mt 19:5) She is me. I am her. We are inseparable. It is somewhat unbelievable how well she truly knows everything about me. The greatest aspect of our relationship is that, in fully giving of ourselves to each other, we experience unconditional love. With that level of love, I have no fear. I am free knowing that as long as I draw breath, she will be committed to me and I her. There is nothing I can do or she could do that would jeopardize that reality. This allows complete honesty in our relationship.

I work hard. As an introvert, my daily interaction with people draws energy from me. Therefore when I return home, I am usually totally exhausted. It is that moment when I first enter the door that my children descend on me like a bunch of vultures to a carcass. As I walk through my house with children hanging from all of my appendages, I am so tempted to hide in a room and close the door for a while to recover.

It is these moments where Elizabeth calls me on to be better than I would be on my own. This time with my kids, hearing about their lives, is the most important thing I do on any given day. Although I would rather hide, they need me. When I battle the demons in my life, especially with the "Religion of Self," she draws me back, she draws me home. She reminds me about the meaning of my life. She reminds me about our community at home and about my responsibility within that "body." She reminds me about my priorities in the big picture. My soul is hers to tend to, and boy, considering how much of a screw up I am, the tending of my soul is a testament to her sainthood. Miraculously, she might just get me to the finish line. In my commitment to her and to my family, I am fulfilling

Looking at that lesson superficially, I thought "Of course I am not God." Then I started evaluating *my* life, *my* priorities, *my* behavior, and *my* beliefs and found that, in many ways, I actually try to *be God* unto myself all the time.

I found I want control of everything. I want to control my time, my environment, my belongings, the people around me, my money, my children, my wife, my job. I wanted the power to justify my behavior. **In the "Religion of Self," there is no greater thought than that *my* opinion is what matters most.** Especially with regard to sin, I wanted to define the Truth for myself. If I fell short of the "bar of perfection" established by Christ, I would set the bar lower for my convenience. After all, we have all heard from our culture "what is true for you is true for you and what is true for me is true for me." I didn't realize at the time that what that statement really says is that there is *no* Truth, we are all just making it up as we go along. Therefore, with this flawed line of thinking, ultimately the Truth is *relative*. If I am a god unto myself, and you are a god unto yourself, then who is right? Where does the Truth lie? Can the Truth be contradictory? If the principle is that everybody's truth is right, is there such a thing as Truth? In reality, mankind has always searched for Truth. When Pontius Pilate was interrogating Christ, even he asked, "What is Truth?"

I am Roman Catholic. I find many within our Faith saying "I am a Catholic but I don't believe in…." These issues include the Church's teaching on fornication (sex outside of the confines of marriage), homosexuality, abortion, divorce, contraception, woman becoming priests, and so forth. Some want a buffet of alternative truths. I want some of this and not some of that. In essence, what I was doing in my youth was making up my own religion, let's call it "Ryanism," whereby I made up truths as I saw fit. What I failed to ask myself was this: if I believe the Church is true in most areas, how did the Church lose its authority in the Truth in areas in which I disagreed?

Many of us live by the standards of behavior we set for ourselves. We make up our own code of morality and we make up our own rules. **If we believe that morality and Truth are relative and individual, we cannot believe in God.** God defines perfection in all areas. He is perfect Love, Mercy, Power, Justice, Knowledge, and Ultimate Reality. **If you really** believe in God, you therefore must believe in *objective* Truth because GOD IS TRUTH!!

In discovering that "There is a God and I am not Him," I began to understand that there is *objective, unadulterated* Truth: Truth that is still true whether I like it or not; Truth that is still true whether or not I have a different opinion; Truth that is still true whether or not I have the ability to live up to that standard. Truth is not a democracy. Truth is not an opinion poll. Truth is *reality*. I have a free will to accept it… or reject it and practice Ryanism. If "There is a God and I am not Him," then there is Truth that transcends the desires of my will and what I prefer to make up on my own.

I am not the first person to have a struggle with this basic principle. We have been trying to be God unto ourselves since the beginning of mankind as described in the Bible, Genesis chapter 3: 1-5

> "Now the serpent was the most cunning of all the animals that the Lord God had made. The serpent asked the woman, "Did God really tell you not to eat from any of the trees in the garden?" The woman answered the serpent: "We may eat of the fruit of the trees in the garden; it is only about the fruit of the tree in the middle of the garden that God said, 'You shall not eat it or even touch it, lest you die.' But the serpent said to the woman: "You certainly will not die! No, God knows well that the moment you eat of it your eyes will be opened and you will BE LIKE GODS WHO WILL KNOW WHAT IS GOOD AND WHAT IS BAD."

Sound familiar? Is this not the same situation we face every day of our lives? The first sin was not merely a sin of disobedience. More significantly, it was the *first "original sin"* whereby Mankind first decided to be "like God." I too, have tasted that apple. I grab that apple with two hands and take a big juicy bite out of it every time I desire to be God unto myself. The deadly spiritual principle of *moral relativism*, the failure to accept the objective Truth of God, entered the world that instant.

Trying to *be God* has been the root of all evil on this planet from the very beginning of civilized man. Genesis was written at least fifteen hundred years prior to the birth of Christ and it was traditionally thought to have been referring to a time four thousand years before Christ. To state this differently, think about how long ago Christ lived before now and what has happened on the earth over the past 2000 years. Moses was nearly that long before Christ and the events he was writing about were that long before him. As I said earlier, the principles of Scripture transcend time. The principles of Scripture are relevant to mankind today. We are literally asking the same questions and are hungry for the Truth. If the principles of Scripture are true, and God is Truth, then in the depth of our soul we can recognize Truth and still learn from Scripture today.

As a consequence of Man's disobedience to God, and, more importantly, the attempt to be God unto ourselves, death entered the world. As I was growing up, I thought of this as only physical death. I have since learned that it is far deeper than that. When we try to be God, we welcome *spiritual* death into our lives. ***Every sin* is rooted in this desire to be God. Every sin is rooted in pride. Every sin is rooted in self.** Sin is ultimately the spiritual sickness that can cause death to our souls.

Here is the good news. In His mercy, justice, and love, God also gives mankind the path out of physical and spiritual death. In the same chapter in Genesis He says to the serpent, "I will put enmity between you and the woman, and between your offspring and hers; He will strike at your head, while you strike at His heel."

God is already laying out a plan for our salvation in the same chapter of Genesis. He is already telling us about the reality of His only beloved Son, His Word, His Truth, entering the world to defeat physical and spiritual death and satisfy divine, eternal justice.

Cardinal Ratzinger, in his last homily prior to becoming Pope Benedict XVI, said "No longer can we live in a world of moral relativism. We have Truth and His name is Jesus Christ!" I heard that line and felt instantly why God would choose him to become pope at that time.

Through the fall of our first parents, Adam and Eve, we have all inherited the desire to *be God* in our own lives. I struggle with this on a daily basis. Not only do I attempt to control everything and everyone around me, I even try to control God. If you think this doesn't apply to you, ask yourself this question: The last time I prayed, what did the prayer sound like? I used to pray "God, heal this person. God, help me get a raise at my job. God, let me get an A on my test. God, make this person leave me alone. God, put an end to my suffering." In these scenarios, who is God? If I was trying to be a god even in my prayer life, how many other places in my life was I failing to allow God to be in control?

In my prayer life, like most of the rest of my life, I wanted to control God. If He didn't jump as high as I requested, I would penalize our relationship with doubt. It was like being in a baseball game and I was the coach telling God (the player) what to do. I have since changed how I pray. If one of my children asks me for junk food all day long, I say "no" to prevent them from getting a stomachache. If the same child asks for a piece of fruit, the answer is always "yes." **God will always answer your prayer if it is spiritually healthy for you.** I have learned to pray for attributes that will strengthen my soul to allow me to be a better disciple of the Lord and hopefully allow me to enter Heaven for eternity. In receiving these attributes, one can have a glimpse of Heaven *now* with daily, lasting joy. My prayers now consist of asking God to give me strength and courage to do His will. This includes requests for inner peace, patience, fortitude, and humility. In praying for others, I pray that they develop a better relationship with the Lord. I pray to more fully understand the Truth. I pray for wisdom in guiding my family. I have learned to also repent and evaluate my life and my actions. Finally, I simply use prayer to praise God and thank Him for everything. Thanksgiving with praise and adoration is the highest form of prayer. A prayer of thanksgiving is the ultimate prayer of trust and acceptance of the journey I am on with God. It is the ultimate prayer that reflects that "There is a God and I am not Him."

One caution: I have learned to be careful about what I ask for in prayer. I have discovered that most of the virtues and attributes I want come at a cost: *suffering.* Fortitude, patience, humility, wisdom, and so forth are frequently acquired by one making mistakes and then humbly learning from them. Through the humility of suffering, one can be honed like a sword that has been shaped through the fiery pain of the furnace. One becomes spiritually strong.

In preparing for a talk I was going to give to teenagers recently, a thought I received in prayer was that I had to *"die to myself."* If my free will is the only thing that is truly my own, what that really means is that *I must die to my will.* I then thought of a scene from the mini-series "Band of Brothers" (2001). The setting was a battlefield in World War II. One soldier was a hero, running in the open, taking enemy fire at every turn to complete his mission. A second soldier was cowering in a ditch, completely paralyzed in fear. The soldier in the ditch finally asked the hero how he had the courage to run through the battlefield. The hero answered, **"Because I am already dead."**

If we could die to ourselves, if we could die to our will, we would lose all of our fear and become "born again" (Jn 3:3) as fearless disciples of Jesus Christ! If our will could simply and only be to serve the Lord at every moment of every day, why would we have fear? Would we fear how others perceive us? Would we worry about having enough material goods or not achieving worldly success? If we truly believed that God is in control and Heaven is our eternal destiny, would we still fear losing a family member or becoming ill? Would we fear loneliness or worry about how our bodies look? Would we even fear physical death?

The solution to living a life where "There is a God and I am not Him" is to *become like a child* in that relationship. As Christ notes in the New Testament (Mt 18:3); "You must become like a child in order to enter the Kingdom of Heaven." A child has no control. A child looks fully and completely to his or her parents for everything throughout his young life. A child is completely and utterly dependent. That childlike innocence and trust allows that child to be free from worry and fear. No longer is there anxiety about tomorrow. No longer is there an unquenchable drive for wealth and power. A child simply exists… wanting to know, love and be with his parents. There is a deep peace and joy in that state of mind. A child truly lives life following the motto "There is a God and I am not Him!"

Dust

"We are dust and unto dust we shall return." This is spoken by the priest when Catholics receive ashes on Ash Wednesday. We say this to remind of us the reality that all of the created matter that we experience through our senses of sight, hearing, taste, smell, and touch is simply "passing through" existence. All of this matter has a finite end point. In the end, everything we experience on Earth is dust. "Vanity of vanities! All things are vanity!"(Ec1:2)

Without God, there is no point. Within the Universe, we are simply dust. Our matter does not hold any innate value. **It is only because of God's love *for us* that we become infinitely valuable.** Part of that infinite value comes from being created "in His image." We were not only created with finite matter, but also His infinite Spirit. "The Lord God formed man out of the clay of the ground and blew into his nostrils the breath of life, and so man became a living being."(Gn2:7) As a potter makes a pot from clay, God created us with matter and gave us Himself through His Spirit to make life as we know it. Through His gift of Himself present in our spirit, He therefore created us "in His image." We are literally His children. Although we are born physically from our parents, we are born spiritually from the "breath of God" with an eternal spirit or soul as His gift of Himself to us. It is because our soul's origin as the "breath of God" that *our soul will last for eternity.*

<u>It is the Cross of Jesus Christ that defines our innate value. The Cross is the key.</u> It is through the divine blood sacrificed for me that the Lord reveals how much He values me. I am the lost sheep that the Shepherd left everything to find. I am of infinite value not because of anything I have done or will ever do. I am of infinite value because I am a child of God and He loves me enough to lay down His life for my sin and

ultimately my salvation. I am made "in His image" and His breath gives me life. *I am of infinite value because the "breath of God" has infinite value.*

Although I am dust and upon dust I shall return, do not think that I am saying that the matter in which I exist means nothing. Look at your hand. Then, *really* look at your hand. Consider how magnificent the creation of our Potter. We have countless cells working continuously at every given moment. Each cell is like a biological entity in and of itself. It grows, metabolizes, walls off infection, has function provided by the nucleus, and structural support. It ultimately dies and is replaced. Each cell works in union with other cells. Each unique cell has a function vital to the support and well-being of the other cells in the body *without our conscious input.*

Our hand has cells composing marrow then bone. The bones have shapes and joints to enable us to have fingers. These bones are stabilized by ligaments and muscles and tendons. We have 2 sets of vessels, bringing blood to and from the cells in the hand to continue providing the hand with oxygen. We have nerves of sensation and nerves of motor impulses to allow our hand to feel and move. We have temperature gauges within the hand and sensors and signals in the blood vessels which regulate how much blood flow is needed in the hand vs. elsewhere. We have fat and skin with oil and sweat glands that keep the cells of the skin healthy and help regulate temperature. We have hair with follicles and keratin in our nails. Every cell in every part I just mentioned is working at every moment of our existence. Each cell works not only individually, but as a piece to a larger whole.

Why the litany of biology? This is just the hand. Think of how our entire physical body is this complicated in every aspect. Every created biological entity in our world is this complicated. I simply sit in awe of the Creator who can design this masterpiece. Analyzing the complexity of the hand also reveals to me how far many will go to try to avoid belief in God. An atheist would literally have to never look at the fantastic creation of this world, starting with himself, and ignore all that is marvelous about his being. An atheist would have to go *out of his way* to believe there is no God.

I accept that I am dust, and regardless of how marvelous this body of mine is, unto dust this body of mine shall return. With this realization, I can accept how small I actually am in the grand scheme of things, especially in comparison to God. I am just dust. I am just clay. With this thought, **I have also come to the conclusion that there is nothing** *more delusional* **than the thought that my personal opinion actually matters in the Truth and Reality of the universe.**

I am presently writing this book on top of a desk. The desk is a reality. If I do not want it to be a desk, does it no longer remain a desk? If I tell everybody it is not a desk, or we all have a vote that we have an opinion that it is not a desk, in Truth, does the desk cease to be a desk? All of our collective opinions are totally and completely irrelevant to Reality.

To state this differently, several years ago during a retreat in Ireland, I had an upstart, rebellious, disrespectful, difficult teenager who was drama incarnate. I am a fisherman of sorts. Not of fish, but of souls. In this case, with this soul, I was deep sea fishing in my little dingy in the storms of the deep, depending completely on God. I have found that although the souls are more difficult to catch in the deep, when caught, they are huge!! I never give up on them because I love them.

This was a big soul. Days into the retreat, despite many telling me to send this "bad apple" home as his negativity was a cancer to the rest of the Body of Christ, the apex of his rebellion was revealed. His grandmother, who was raising him recently died. He was mad at God so he screamed in his most radical, northern Irish accent, "I dooooown't beleeeve in Gooooddd!!!" He thought that would upset me. I smiled and stated, "Whether or not you believe in Him does not make Him disappear. You have simply chosen to leave Reality. And thus, you have chosen to therefore live in illusion and a lie." This Truth seemingly hit him between the eyes. As his mouth hung open in surprise, he stopped and settled down and ultimately join us for the rest of the week.

God is Reality. God is Truth. He does not cease to be in any way because of *our* **opinion of Him!!!** This *delusion of grandeur*, this belief that our opinion actually matters started with the first bite of the apple in the Garden of Eden, "and you will be LIKE GOD and know what is good and bad."(Gn3:5) In short, when we eat the apple, we will forget that there is a God and I am not Him. In short, we will forget that we are just dust. In short, we will forget that the root of all wisdom is "fear of the Lord," (knowing and understanding our place in the universe; that we are dust and He is God.)

It took finding the Meaning of Life before I realized that money, diplomas, trophies, and accolades are all dust. I then had to ask, *what lasts?* **Relationships are the only things that are not dust. Relationships are the only things that endure forever. The Trinity is relationship. Love is relationship. GOD IS RELATIONSHIP!**

That is why the bar of perfection in Truth, the Law, is boiled down to 2 statements, "Love your God with your whole heart, mind and strength and love your neighbor as yourself" (because your neighbor is also created in the image and likeness of God as the breath of God is in them.) (Mk12:30) At the moment of our death when we are standing naked in front of God, do you believe any of the dust we cared so much about here on earth will matter? Do you believe piles of money, trophies, awards, degrees, or any part of dust will have any remote use to us at that moment? No. The ultimate question is obvious and simple; did we choose to spend our short time on Earth to develop a relationship with God and the breath of God in others, or not?

How do I build relationships? By serving. Sacrificial love. Death to self! I always seemed to think 2 dimensionally when listening to Jesus in the Gospel. "The first shall be last and the last shall be first in the Kingdom of Heaven."(Mk 9:35) When I was in grade school, I literally thought that this meant I should not fight to be first in line for things. What that really means is **by serving each other, through sacrificial love, we are making decisions free from self, free from the Fall.** In serving each other, we create and enhance relationships with each other and therefore with God.

How many of us have 900 "friends" on Facebook? How many of those friends would volunteer to help you this weekend if you had to move? Other than sending frowning emojis of condolence, how many would physically show up and visit you if you were in the hospital? Who are the servants among us? Who are our real friends? When I moved into my first house, a friend of mine volunteered to help me to put up a fence in the backyard in order to keep my children contained in the yard. (Yes, watching my children is like trying to herd cats and fences are most helpful. I am thinking of upgrading to military drones or implanting GPS devices!) That simple selfless act of service brought our friendship to a whole new level. It built a lasting relationship. **Sacrificial love is the antithesis to the "Religion of Self."**

"What you do unto the least of these, you do unto me."(Mt25:40) Living life shedding the shackles of our senses frees us from the "Religion of Self," the "Religion of Individualism." In serving each other, we can truly experience Church, the Body of Christ – God. Only then can we see God with the essence of our being, not just our physical eyes. Only then we can truly serve each other as if they are Jesus to us. Only then, in that relationship with God can we stand before Him naked in our death and have the only thing that endures, our relationship with Him. Only then have we become innocent children once again.

Sin

One day I was speaking to a bunch of priests and I was asked; "Why are so many people choosing not to attend Mass?" My strongly sarcastic answer startled him and most of the room. I replied, "Didn't you know that *everybody* goes to Heaven?" I have been attending very regular Mass for many, many years and have never heard from the pulpit any serious discussions about Hell.

Over the past 50 years, Hell seems to have become a bad word. I am not proposing fire and brimstone craziness. I am simply noting that when the possibility of Hell is never discussed, most people automatically think that everybody goes to Heaven. **If that is the case, if Hell does not exist, then we do NOT have a God that loves us because He is *forcing* us to be with Him for eternity. If Hell does not exist, we have no free will and we have no meaning to our lives. If Hell does not exist, then why would we need the grace of the cross through the Eucharist?** Why would we need Mass? Why would we need church? Why seek redemption? Why not be god unto ourselves in the "Religion of Self?"

No, in Truth, *if* we have a God that loves us and is not a slave master, Hell *must* exist. Discussion about Hell is actually a discussion about the *love* of God, because in giving us a free will, He gives us the freedom of *not* loving Him. In giving us a free will, because He loves us, He gives us the freedom of not being with Him. Because His love of us entails our freedom, He endures the pain of separation throughout all of eternity as some of His own children can choose separation from Him. Imagine your own child never choosing to come home to want to know you, love you, or have relationship with you. Imagine giving up your own life on a cross for your child, yet that child uses their freedom to choose eternal death and separation from you anyway. Multiply that pain times infinity and you will understand how much our God longs for us.

If the meaning of life is to choose God, then sin is the alternative choice. Sin is 'missing the mark' regarding the purpose of our life. Sin can be acts, thoughts, or omissions that lead us away from our eternal destination of Heaven.

The root of all sin is pride. It is because of pride that I try to be God unto myself. It is because of pride that I often forget that "There is a God and I am not Him." It is through pride that I want control. Pride always comes before our fall from grace.

To reiterate, if God gave us our lives and our free will to choose whether or not we want to be with Him forever, then there has to be a place we could alternatively choose that would be *absent* of God. That alternative place is called Hell. Imagine a place where there is no Truth, no Standard, no Good, no Beauty, no Order, no Hope, no Charity, no Love, no Mercy, no Justice, and no Light. Imagine every person within this place thinking *they* were God, and, through pride, living the "Religion of Self" to its fullest. Imagine the utter loneliness in a place absent of all community. Imagine the hopelessness in a place you know will never improve for all eternity.

Many ask: If we have such a loving God, how could He ever "send" anyone to Hell? I believe that He doesn't. What is Heaven? Relationship with God. Relationship with the Trinity (which is eternal relationship between the Father, Son, and Holy Spirit). Relationship with the breath of God in others. Family. Community. Church.

When we use our free will to *choose* a life of self, self, self, self, and ultimately self, the natural end to the path of self simply continues on throughout all of eternity. Again, it is actually through His *love* for us that He has given us free will, to choose whether or not we want to be in His presence forever. It is because He loves us that He does not force us to be with Him. If we don't want to be with Him, we therefore choose for ourselves to be our own god and thus we choose Hell; we choose separation from Him. "In the end, God will give you what you want." (St. Francis De Sales). Recall Genesis Chapter 3 – The moment you eat of it your eyes will be open and YOU WILL BE LIKE GODS WHO KNOW WHAT

IS GOOD AND WHAT IS BAD. **Remember, all who want to be God get their own kingdom absent of the true God. We call that Hell.**

I have had the privilege of hearing about many "near death experiences." A vast majority of the stories I have heard have had experiences that are very, very similar to each other. All of them describe experiences of Heaven or Hell. One thing that repeatedly sticks out about those who describe a near death experience in Hell is the *eternal* nature of it. There is eternal remorse knowing that they wasted this relatively short period of existence called our life. There is eternal remorse in Hell knowing with full consciousness that it will never, ever, ever get better. Eternity is a long time.

My father taught me a lot about the Truth. One analogy he used made a lot of sense to me. Have you ever seen a light bulb on without a shade over it? It is really bright, even hard to look at. It also gives off heat. Imagine God is like that light bulb, always on, giving light and warmth to the world. Imagine sin is like a shade. Every time we sin we choose to place a shade on that light bulb. The light is still on but it is not quite as bright nor is it quite as warm. Then we sin again and choose to place another shade on that light. Pretty soon our spiritual relationship with the Lord becomes darker and colder. It seems to become easier for us to sin and it seems easier to place more shades on that light. Slowly but surely, we soon forget that God, The Light, is on. After putting so many shades on Him, we have now chosen a dark, cold, place for ourselves. We become accustomed to the darkness to the point where, if God is shining through another person, that light hurts our spiritual eyes and we flee from that light. That dark place is Hell.

I have met many people in my life who are already experiencing Hell, this separation from God right here on Earth. They are so enslaved by their sin that they have made a personal Hell for themselves. They become accustomed to the dark. These individuals enjoy the blinding light of the Holy Spirit shining in others about as much as I enjoyed my mother flipping on my bedroom light at 7am on a Saturday morning when I was a teenager. The light hurts their spiritual eyes.

To further understand being trapped in Hell on Earth, talk to any addict or drug abuser. Talk to any person who gave up family and community for wealth, power, and glorification of self. What you will find are individuals who are in the darkness, starving for the next fix of their addiction, feeling enslaved, alone, and utterly empty. Some in the dark are repulsed and lash out against the light and grace offered by others. If you truly allow the Lord to work through you, those in darkness will strive to put you on a cross. Just ask the martyrs. Some, however, are memorized and drawn to that same light, repenting and desiring to start anew. These individuals become God's saints.

The good news about this life is that the light of God is still on. **As long as we still have breath, there is always hope for returning to a relationship with God.** It reminds me of one of Jesus' most well- known parables.

> "A man had two sons, and the younger son said to his father, 'Father, give me the share of your estate that should come to me.' So the father divided the property between them. After a few days, the younger son collected all his belongings and set off to a distant country where he squandered his inheritance on a life of dissipation. When he had freely spent everything, a severe famine struck that country, and he found himself in dire need. So he hired himself out to one of the local citizens who sent him to his farm to tend the swine. He longed to eat his fill of the pods on which the swine fed, but nobody gave him any. Coming to his senses he thought, 'How many of my father's hired workers have more than enough food to eat, but here am I, dying from hunger. I shall get up and go to my father and I shall say to him, "Father, I have sinned against heaven and against you. I no longer deserve to be called your son; treat me as you would treat one of your hired workers."' So he got up and went back to his father. While he was still a long way off, his father caught sight of him, and was filled with compassion. He ran to his son, embraced him and kissed him. His son said to him "Father, I have sinned against heaven and against you; I no longer deserve to be called your son." But his father ordered his servants, "Quickly bring the finest robe and put it on him; put a ring on his finger and sandals on

his feet. Take the fatted calf and slaughter it. Then let us celebrate with a feast, because this son of mine was dead, and has come to life again; he was lost, and has been found." (Lk 15:11)

I see myself in the beginning of this parable living the "Religion of Self." This spiritual "teenager" chooses to leave his home. He decides to leave the authority of his household, to be a god unto himself. He leaves his family community and the relationship he had with his father, essentially saying he wished his father was dead so he could take his inheritance.

This teenager then "set off to a distant country," leaving his land and local community. He then "squandered his inheritance on a life of dissipation" essentially choosing to end his relationship with God and leaves his religious community. He wanted control. He wanted to be god to himself. He did not want to answer to anything or anybody.

Once famine struck, he was forced to work at a pig farm in order to survive. This is ironic because, as a kosher Jew, there would be no lower place on earth than working with swine. He was not only working with the pigs, "he longed to eat his fill of the pods on which the swine fed." Symbolically, he was becoming like a pig himself, the most detestable of all creatures during that time.

It is at this moment in the story when the teenager experiences *humility* for the first time. Again, pride is the root of all sin. Humility is the opposite of pride. The moment this youth became more humble through self-evaluation and admission of his error, he began having clarity of thought. His journey of life was instantly turned around and restarted in a positive direction. This turn-around is called conversion of heart through *repentance*.

This teenager had the courage to act on this newfound humility and went back home. His father had never given up on him. **THE LIGHT WAS STILL ON.** Once the son left, the father waited, looking into the distance, hoping for his son to **CHOOSE** to return home. His father saw his son in the distance and ran to him and embraced him, even in his son's 'pigness.' His father was overjoyed at the return of his son and his household (Heaven) was open to him.

God is waiting for you right now. He is ready and eager to embrace each of us in our 'pigness' and welcome us into the kingdom of heaven. All that is needed is *humility* and the desire to 'return home.' We must die to our will. We must become like children, innocent and trusting and longing for home.

Confession

Have you ever had a bad fight with someone you deeply love? Whenever I happen to be the bonehead who is too stuck on my ideas, desires, and self, throughout the entire argument and afterward I feel awful. I get this queasy feeling in my gut like I would have if I were car sick. If there is no quick resolution, I can harbor a prolonged sense of guilt, anger at myself for fighting in the first place, and resentment to whomever I argued with. **There is nothing emotionally or spiritually healthy about unresolved conflict that damages the only thing that matters; relationship with God or the 'breath of God' in others.**

When I sin, I am in conflict with God and whoever I am hurting. Even if I sin in private, I am still hurting both my relationship with God and others because I belong to the "Body of Christ." I do not exist in a vacuum. We are called to greatness and when we fail, even in the dark, we are failing in that calling. If one part of the body is ill, the whole body suffers. It is like trying to walk with a rock in your shoe. Such a small thing can cause such great distraction of purpose for the rest of the body. The whole body suffers when one of its parts is not working to its potential.

Often, I then experience the same moment of pause that the prodigal son had in his 'pigness.' Through evaluation of self in humility, I long to go back to re-establish the relationship I challenged. I long to go home. The Catholic sacrament of Confession is a bastion of grace established at the Cross where we can receive that grace through repentance. Confession is the opportunity for God to embrace us and forgive us as the prodigal son's father embraced him. All Catholic sacraments are physical manifestations of a spiritual reality. Every Catholic sacrament was established by Christ himself. The sacrament of Confession is no different.

Jesus said to them again, "Peace be with you. As the Father has sent me, so I send you." And when he had said this, he breathed on them and said to them, "Receive the Holy Spirit. Whose sins you forgive are forgiven them, and whose sins you retain are retained."(Jn20:21)

Note, Jesus did not say, "Tell everybody to confess their sins directly to God on their own." He sent his apostles out as himself, giving them divine *authority* over sin.

Recall when I described God as like a light bulb that is always on and our sin is like putting a lampshade on that light bulb. Confession is our choosing to allow God to take a bazooka and blow up that shade, allowing his light, warmth, and grace to freely flow back into our lives without hindrance. Imagine having very dirty glasses. As you wear them, you do not realize how dirty they are. When you take them off and hold them to the light, every particle of filth becomes clear. Through the evaluation of conscience prior to our confession, Confession is holding up our 'spiritual glasses' to the light of God.

Confession not only repairs a damaged relationship with God, it heals our relationship with the "Body of Christ." That is why we don't just say sorry to God alone in prayer. The Catholic priest is "in persona Christi" in the confessional: Jesus Christ actually present. The priest then represents both Christ's divinity and humanity in the Confessional – representing both God and "the Body of Christ," His Church.

Several things must be present for absolution to take effect. First, I must be sorry for what I did. Second, it has to actually be a sin (yes, you heard me right. Half the time my wife goes to confess something, the priest sends her home telling her he is not needed). Third, I have to intend on not falling again. Finally, I must avoid the "near occasion" of sin. Before receiving absolution by a priest, a Catholic normally recites a beautiful prayer called the "Act of Contrition."

"Oh my God I am heartily sorry for having offended thee, and I detest of all my sin because of thy just punishment, but most of all because I offended thee my God, who art all good and deserving of all my love. I firmly resolve, with the help of thy grace, to sin no more and *to avoid the near occasion of sin.*"

I have found that I am far more likely to fall into sin in certain situations more than others. Growing up, before my time was absorbed with caring for my family, certain people I associated with would lead me into situations where I would be weak. The reality is that regardless of these bad associations, I am an extremely weak man anyway. Those weaknesses would simply be exploited when I was around those specific people. With this recognition, I try not to "play chicken" with sin. I try not to even place myself in the vicinity where anything bad might happen.

In my profession in medicine, I am surrounded with physically beautiful, lonely, and aggressive woman. My awesome wife, recognizing my challenges declared one day that "I was her lion." I responded, "No dear, I am your gazelle. I see trouble and run my little tail off!"

An alcoholic probably should not hang out in a bar. A smoker probably should not hand out in the smoking section. A gambler probably should not loiter in a casino. I need to avoid situations where I am most apt to be weak in all aspects of my life. Satan knows what buttons to push. His only objective is to draw me away from the mercy of the Cross. His only objective is my eternal soul. Just because I love God, I am in no way immune. Satan seems to spend more of his efforts on me than he used to and he is a worthy and difficult adversary. My only defense is recognizing my weakness, seriously avoiding the occasions where I might be most tempted to sin, and finally, recognizing my absolute dependence on the mercy and care of God. I depend on the Cross! I often fall but have no problem crying out for my angels and saints in Heaven to spiritually intercede and help me back on my feet through the grace of the Cross in Confession.

Confession offers very specific grace. It not only offers sacramental grace as the mercy of God. It offers specific grace *to avoid falling to the same sin*. Confession is a very good way to break bad habits.

Again, I am not writing this chapter because I have somehow mastered the secret of avoiding a sinful life. In reality I battle sin and often lose every day. I am usually the guy who gets to talk to my RCIA class about sin because I am the "expert" on the subject through too much experience.

When I was in college, I was in the confessional with a super holy priest. He stepped foot onto my college at the Franciscan University of Steubenville as the vocational director and, as a result of his impact, in one year, over 50 young men strongly considered the priesthood. He was the kind of guy that when he entered the room, you would feel the hair on your arm rising. At one point I was in the confessional with him bargaining about my sins. I wanted to know if certain sins of mine were classified as venial sins or mortal sins. As I continued to bargain with him, he finally sat back, smiled, and stated, **"Ryan, for those who LOVE the Lord, there is no difference between venial and mortal sins, because in both cases, you are hurting your relationship with the Lord."**

That was a profound, life-changing statement for me. Why was I always trying to do the minimum? Why did I aspire to be the guy who just sneaks into Heaven at the last minute? Had I not learned that the sin I was still secretly hoping to continue, was hurting my relationship with God? As I noted before, some sins made me momentarily "happy" but would then leave a spiritual hang-over and would certainly never provide lasting joy. I was literally fighting to be able to continue having spiritual cancer in my life. What foolish justifications I have used throughout my life to continue being spiritually ill. It is like a smoker saying he is 'trying' to quit as he still carries a pack of cigarettes in his pocket. Anyone who fights to continue sin *is a slave* to sin.

I have learned that prayer and grace from the sacraments, especially the Eucharist and Confession with a priest, is the best medicine. Sin is like a spiritual cancer and as a spiritual cancer patient, I look forward to the day where I can be free from this disease. In Christ, I feel myself getting stronger. In my journey with Jesus, I am feeling healthier all of the time. Lord, free me of my addiction of self. Free me from the slavery of sin. I depend on you to hold my hand during the difficult parts of my life that I am tempted to wander off your path. Fill me with a thirst to be the man you hoped I could be when you created me. I love you.

God Will Take
You as You Are

I am one of nine children. One of my six sisters grew up being an all-star. She was good at everything. She got straight A's in school. She excelled socially, athletically, musically, and even spiritually. One day she tinkered with bulimia. This rapidly became a severe addiction. It put severe strains on my family financially, mentally, but especially emotionally. Everybody wanted to help her but we just couldn't find a solution. It was like witnessing a member of your family who you fiercely love drowning in your sight, not reaching up to allow you to pull her out. She was in and out of hospitals without success. She experienced guilt and started hurting herself. She began to drink alcohol daily to forget her pain. Ultimately, she entered that dark, lonely, empty place I spoke of earlier: a type of Hell. She would flee from and lash out against those with the light as the light would be blinding in her darkness. She continued on this self-destructive, suicidal-like path for nearly a decade until every moment of her day was consumed by binging, purging, and drinking. She was at her absolute lowest point. She was in the state of despair. She bought into the lie of *Satan's view of her identity*: a lowly, sinful creature *unworthy* of God's love.

At her lowest moment I sat down to talk with her and she was finally desperate enough to listen. She told me that she believed her sins were so awful that she was convinced she was destined for Hell. I responded that the only person who was keeping her from returning to the house of the Lord was herself. What an arrogant thought to believe that the God of the universe, the God of all creation, the God of life and love wouldn't have the capacity to forgive her sins – That the blood of God Himself in sacrifice was not enough! I told her to stop fixating on her weakness and her faults and start focusing on the solution which is a relationship with the Lord. **God will take you as you are.** I told her to work on that relationship and put no priority above that. She might still struggle with bulimia and abuse alcohol the rest of her life until she dies but God still loves her and wants to be with her above all things. He certainly is not the one that would ever fixate on her faults.

She then focused all of her energy on her relationship with Him and spent over a month in upstate New York in a Franciscan hermitage. This gave her the opportunity to be free from her physical addictions while redeveloping a relationship with God. She went through a "spiritual boot camp," and for the first time in ten years, experienced hope and the love of God. She was once again able to dive into His light and stay there. Through constant prayer and time spent in front of Jesus in Eucharistic Adoration, her demons of bulimia and alcohol abuse have been controlled for over 15 years.

Years ago, I was eating my breakfast as I always do, sharing it bite for bite with my daughter Grace on my knee. I just sat there watching her eat. She was so utterly content. She had complete trust in me. She did not have a care in the entire world. She just wanted to know me, love me, and be with me like that forever. It was so simple. At that moment I felt like how God must feel toward us. I felt totally at peace and, again, experienced true joy.

It dawned on me then why God allowed us to have children. If the meaning of life is to choose God, He could have just made us in our twenties and we could have made the "choice" for eternity and have been finished. Instead, as stated in Genesis: He made us "in His image." He allows us to co-create with Him and allows us to participate in bringing life into this world. I used to frequently ask "what does God want from me?" I think in allowing us to have a family, He has given us a pretty good clue.

God has allowed us to have children so we could have an idea about how He feels about us. Although our relationship with our children is imperfect, and our relationship with our own earthly parents is imperfect, our relationship with God is still very similar. The difference is that His parental relationship with us *is* perfect.

I want my children to be good. I want my children to be upright in character and honor. I want them to be honest, compassionate, caring, helpful, respectful, appreciative, and I want them to always try their best. I want them to live to their potential and to find lasting joy. I want them to uplift everyone around them. I want to be proud of them. I try to focus on their strengths and, if they are truly contrite, I really don't remember their weaknesses. I love them deeply. I believe I would die for them. All I really ever want from them as their father is for them to get to Heaven and *to know me, love me, and freely choose to be with me, even when they are out of the house and they no longer have to.* Is our Father in Heaven so different?

When my son does something at home that I am not thrilled about, I feel sad. The good news is that as long as he is at home, we can work through anything. We have a relationship where I believe he knows I would always forgive him, no matter what. There is no sin he can commit in my household that would cause me to banish him. The greatest tragedy would be if he were to ever *doubt my love* for him and choose to no longer be in my home. As welcome as he would be, he could choose to no longer continue our relationship. I couldn't force him to know me, love me, or want to be with me for eternity. I would still love him. I would long for his return.

Are you home with the Lord? Do you long to know Him, love Him, and be with Him for eternity? You still draw breath. There is still time. God will take you as you are.

The Cross

Imagine having a gift that is so special, so spectacular that it took your very life to create it. Imagine this gift was a rope that dangled down into a dark pit where your very own children were temporarily trapped. All they had to do was grab that rope by dying to themselves and thereby opening themselves to this infinite grace transmitted through the rope. That is the cross of Christ.

"He said to them, you belong to what is below. I belong to what is above. You belong to this world, but I do not belong to this world. That is why I told you that you will die in your sins. For if you do not believe that I AM, you will die in your sins."(Jn8:23)

Why was atonement for our sins necessary? It is because we have a God who is Just. Our sin committed has eternally challenged infinite justice. With our first sin, there was injury to an eternal, infinite relationship between man and God. There must be a consequence to our action, not because of what Adam and Eve did in sin, but because of Whom it is they offended by that sin. Their sin created an eternal chasm in the relationship between man and God because God is Infinite. It was through our Fall that we fell into this pit.

Do you believe God is Infinite? Do you believe God is Just? Do you believe God is Mercy? Our forefathers believed in these attributes of God. In the Old Testament, after the fall of man through the first sin of Adam and Eve, man routinely offered sacrifice to God. This was true with Abel, Abraham, and Moses. Why did man sacrifice? It is through the blood of the sacrifice that man would hope to receive finite atonement for their sin. The reason the sacrifice was temporary was that we were sacrificing finite animals to atone for *in*finite Justice.

Throughout the entire Old Testament, the Hebrews repeatedly entered a covenant, an eternal oath, with God. Repeatedly, the Hebrews would break this covenant. It was so bad that God often referred to His chosen people as his "unfaithful spouse." The reason this arrangement was problematic was that His chosen people were human and He is God. They could never live up to His perfect standard. Therefore, the only sacrifice that can truly satisfy infinite or divine justice would be if our atonement was made through divine sacrifice. That divine sacrifice could only be given by God alone. Said best by Dr. Scott Hahn; "God would have to pay a debt He did not owe because man owed a debt he could not pay."

Two of Christ's missions on this planet, as we have discussed, include first coming down from Heaven to show us the "perfect choice." As the Way, the Truth, and the Life, Christ provided a roadmap of perfect behavior in order for us to foster a relationship with God the Father and hopefully join Him throughout eternity. The second and more important mission of Christ was to be the Divine Sacrifice. In the person of Jesus Christ, and through his crucifixion and resurrection, God has once again revealed His justice, mercy, and love.

Protestants frequently argue that all one has to do is "believe that Jesus died for their sins" and they will be saved. "Whoever believes and is baptized will be saved, whoever does not believe will be condemned."(Mk16:16)

My response is Satan believes that Jesus died for the sins of the world and he is not in Heaven. Do the 'saved' no longer possess a free-will? Are the 'saved' no longer accountable for their actions?

Belief is not simply acknowledging Truth. What does belief mean? "Faith of itself, if it does not have works, is dead."(Jm2:17) Belief is not just knowing *about* something. **Belief is incorporation of faith into the *action* of our lives.** That does NOT mean that we can *earn* our way into Heaven through good works. **The Cross is the only font of infinite grace. It is ONLY through the cross of Jesus Christ that humanity can be saved, as his blood is divine!** However, we are *only able to receive* that infinite grace of the Cross through the death of ourselves, which then leads to good works. **The root of all good works is sacrificial love. The root of all good works is death to self!** Good works, prayer, and the sacraments are the vehicles of grace that open our lives up to the infinite grace of the Cross. It is through good works that we can grab onto that 'divine rope' given to us at the Cross, where our God can then pull us into his presence in Heaven throughout all of eternity. For those who did not grow up in the "Fullness of the Truth" through the Catholic Church, the "Fullness of the Truth in Jesus Christ," His divine blood on the cross is objectively needed to save all. He did not just die for believers. All entering Heaven, with or without their knowledge, could only enter Heaven through His divine sacrifice.

The Cross not only reveals to mankind the truth of God's justice and love. **The Cross is God's mercy.** There is only one sin in scripture that cannot be forgiven. That is "Blasphemy against the Holy Spirit."

"Therefore, I say to you, every sin and blasphemy will be forgiven people, but blasphemy against the Spirit will not be forgiven."(Mt12:31) Why? Because the Holy Spirit is Mercy! The only way we do not receive the infinite grace of the cross is because we can choose not to accept God's mercy. It is the same sin my sister was flirting with when she thought her sins were "too big for God." God is a gentleman. He will not impose his mercy upon us because mercy is a gift. In dying to ourselves, in dying to our will, we can therefore open our heart and lives to the infinite mercy of the Cross.

One of the greatest ways to open up the infinite font of mercy from the Cross is *to be merciful* to others. In the "Our Father," the prayer Christ himself taught the Church, we pray "Forgive us our trespasses *as* we forgive those who trespass against us…" **There is a direct relationship with the amount of mercy we offer to others to the capacity of mercy we then allow ourselves to receive from God.**

Allowing God to shower us with the grace of the cross in our lives through miracles can only happen if we have faith.

"Jesus said to them, 'A prophet is *not* without honor except in his native place and among his own kin and in his own house.' So he was not able to perform any mighty deeds there, apart from curing few sick people by laying hands on them. He was amazed at their lack of faith."(Mk6:4)

Miracles are a gift from God. He cannot give us this gift of a miracle unless we are willing to receive it. Faith will allow us to receive the miracle of Truth. Truth is God and God is Mercy. Through faith, we can therefore receive the miraculous grace of the Cross, we can therefore receive God's mercy.

The other day I was watching a television program on National Geographic about the universe. There is thought to be more stars in the universe than grains of sand on the entire Earth. The magnitude of the universe is incomprehensible to our human brain.

Thinking about these facts reminds me about how small I am. I am like an ant—no, even less. I am like the smallest particle of dust.

I spent this past Christmas meditating on the reality that the God of this universe, the God of these billions of galaxies and trillions upon trillions of stars, loved me so much that He became man: God became dust. Not only did the God of the universe become dust, He allowed Himself to be born in a stable: He allowed Himself to be the lowest form of dust. I, like the myriads of angels, shepherds, wise men, Joseph and Mary, can only stand in wonderment at the humility of this God.

Not only did God become dust, but He allowed this dust to torture Him, and ultimately to hang Him on a cross. I simply cannot conceive of the degree of love God has for me. This whole story seems really insane. It goes well beyond my reasoning capacity to try and remotely grasp the insane love that God has for me. I sit and stare at the cross and, in the end, I can only praise Him.

What is even more insane is that this God of the universe would have completed this mission if it were to only save *me*. Christ frequently talks about a shepherd dropping everything to search for one lost sheep. It is much like the God of the universe dropping everything to make sure He found *me* and brought *me* home.

I imagine Satan tormenting Jesus in the Garden of Gethsemane on the eve before His death, whispering in his ear, "Are you sure you want to go through with this? Think of how many people will not accept the grace of your divinely shed blood as a result of their pride and conceit. You will be tortured and crucified in vain.

I imagine Christ at that moment, defiantly resisting temptation as He thought of you and me, hoping in *our choice* for salvation. It is thoughts like this that cause me to find myself madly in love with Jesus Christ, *my* Savior.

Christ did not die to fulfill some abstract distant idea. He died for *ME*! In *my* sin He allowed *me* to beat Him. He stood still as I scourged the flesh from His body. He didn't fight back when I slapped Him. He stood with utter dignity as I spit in His face. He didn't cry out as I pressed a crown of thorns into His scalp. He simply closed His eyes when I drove nails through His hands and feet. He looked into my eyes as I raised Him up to suffocate on that cross.

It is through this same cross that He wipes away the tears from my soul. It is through His shed blood that He forgives me, embraces me, kisses me, and welcomes me home to the eternal feast. I love Him, I love Him, I love Him.

The Holy Spirit

This will be an advanced chapter. I am going to tiptoe on the edge of what is known. Please bear with me. I am trying to communicate with language that expresses a state of being and understanding which, by default, our language is limited and imperfect.

Catholics believe in the Holy Trinity: Father, Son, and Holy Spirit. As I am the father to my children, and the son to my father, and the spouse of my wife, I have 3 different perspectives, but I am the same, singular man. God is three unique "persons" yet remains one God.

Up to this point, we have been focusing on God the Father in creation and His son Jesus Christ. The Holy Spirit is the energy, the action, the power, and the breath of God. As a child is the walking, talking manifestation of the love between husband and wife, the Holy Spirit is the walking, talking manifestation of the love shared between the Father and the Son throughout all of eternity, so much so, that this energy of love itself becomes a unique person.

The Holy Spirit as God's action is more of a verb than a noun. God is Truth. God is Reality. God is Life. God is Mercy. God is Beauty. God is Justice. God is Relationship. God is Love.

God, by His nature of being Love is life producing. Otherwise, God wouldn't be God. It is this attribute of God's life-giving existence that the Holy Spirit is a part of everything that has a soul, and to a lesser extent, everything that uses energy. When God breathed life into us, He was giving us a bit of His energy, making us truly His sons and daughters in His image and likeness. It is because of His breath in us, that we, therefore, have an eternal soul or consciousness. This breath of God in us, our soul, is therefore immortal because *His breath cannot cease to exist.* That is why we don't disappear once we die. We just change form and will either exist for eternity in the presence of the Father or not. In other words, that is the basic teaching of our Church regarding the eternal nature of Heaven and Hell.

Our souls, although now unique to us in our existence, live and breathe and exist only due to the energy supplied to it by God, and for the sake of this discussion, the Holy Spirit is the breath of God. Without this energy, without the Holy Spirit, we would not be conscious. Without this energy, life would not exist. Thank you, Holy Spirit! We depend on you!!

Although the Holy Spirit gives life to everything that has life, God cannot be love without giving us the freedom to choose to accept or reject His love. God has given us this life right now, this blink of eternity's eye for us to make a choice on where we would like to spend eternity. He gives us flesh and a free will. With that comes the freedom to be the antithesis of God and choose evil and refuse to love and refuse to forgive. With this comes selfishness, refusal to cherish relationships, to destroy, to hate, to lie and to live in lies. God gives us the freedom through pride to be God unto ourselves. However, in this time of trial, our Valley of Tears, our time of the Flesh, although there is a veil that separates us from Him directly because of our sin and fallen state, He is still present. His Holy Spirit still dwells in our soul.

When I was young, my mom would always say that the Holy Spirit lives in each one of us. To the extent that "God's breath" is in me and I have, therefore, become immortal with that breath, that Holy Spirit, I have a soul. **We also have a will that God allows to have *command over* the Holy Spirit in our soul. GOD IS HUMBLE!!** *God allows us to kill the action of the Holy Spirit in our lives.* Through our egos, through our pride, we can snuff out a life of grace. He allows us in our sin, with our killing of the Holy Spirit, to crucify our God repeatedly. He allows that because he loves us. "Forgive them for they do not know what they are doing." (LK 23:34)

Imagine we are all like stained glass. God created us, He shines through us, and we have been created differently than our brothers and sisters. We are unique and individual. We can make our glass dirty, our portion of this great masterpiece of God, and not allow God to shine through us to the world, or we can be clean and live to our potential in this Body of Christ.

So to review – The Holy Spirit dwells in all of us in our soul. We have a will that God has permitted to contain and crucify that Spirit. We have been given the power of God by God, if we want to, to completely inactivate the Holy Spirit within us.

Ok, let's say we are tired of crucifying God in our lives. How do we activate the Holy Spirit within us? Imagine God is invisible ink throughout the pages of our soul. The Holy Spirit is the reagent, the necessary element to activate that invisible ink so we can see it.

So, how do we activate the Holy Spirit? We need to first understand that There is a God and I am not Him. This is the Motto of Camp Veritas. **There is a God and I am not Him is the source of all wisdom.** Our Catholic Faith is a faith of receptivity. We must die to our will so we can hear the Truth! We must die to our Ego. We must die to ourselves and give ourselves completely to God. We must be born again in Him!

All human beings have "natural lives." Lives that exist. The Holy Spirit is in us enough to give us our lives. The day you can truly become "Reborn in the Spirit" is the day the Holy Spirit who already resides in you takes increasing action. It is the day we can become, with our death, more like Him. To become *supernatural*. **To become more like God because He has been given the permission by our death to be set loose in our lives.** You uncork your *Supernatural* potential, because God has been given permission to take over.

There are a number of ways God has given us to become "Supernatural," to allow His grace to shine through us, and to truly become His instrument. Through our baptism, God has given us this potential of "supernatural lives." Baptism invites us into this supernatural family of the Trinity. It pours the chocolate into the glass of milk. The remaining sacraments stir up the Holy Spirit that exists in all of us. They stir the chocolate milk. Through the grace of the sacraments, we become Superman, or the children of God that God has built us to be. The sacraments are bastions of infinite grace – *but proportionate to our state of receptivity.* The sacraments are critical in this awakening. It is manna for the journey in this lifetime of dying to ourselves.

When one dies to himself, allowing the Holy Spirit within themselves to be set loose, the veil of separation between God and man becomes much thinner. Then, and only then, one can tear the scales from their eyes and truly see. They can truly start to appreciate the Holy Spirit in the life around them. From the beauty of life in nature, to the beauty of life within each other. One no longer looks at their neighbor as their sin. Instead, the Holy Spirit in me senses; it feels the Holy Spirit in others. Those on fire in the Spirit can recognize each other because one can recognize genuine joy... A light in the darkness.

One filled with the light of the Holy Spirit can also recognize those who suck the life, light, and energy out of the room. We all know a person who acts like the cancer in a group setting, filled with negativity, gossip, jealousy, envy, revenge, vanity, and hatred. I have patients like this. Through "Discernment of Spirits" (1 Cor 12:10), I can *feel* their negative energy, their "demon."

One can recognize the Holy Spirit by its fruits: Fortitude, charity, patience, kindness, self - control, faithfulness, fortitude, purity, courage, peace, and joy. Notice, happiness is not a fruit of the Spirit.

What is happiness? What is the difference between happiness and peace and joy? So many times, the world says, "Do whatever makes you happy." That is actually a lie perpetuated by Satan himself!!!

Happiness is the fleeting, temporary feeling one gets from the things of this world, the things of this time in our Valley of Tears, the short game. ***Happiness is not a state of being.*** By definition, it comes from a good cup of coffee, winning the lottery, one's sport teams winning, moments of triumph, achieving a worldly goal, but sometimes happiness is experienced in sin. The temptation of all sin is the search for happiness, albeit temporary. The excitement of the wealth, the lust, the power.... Whatever is your vice or your addiction.

It is through this drive for happiness where all addiction springs forth. Imagine a smoker – they smoke to give themselves a temporary moment of relaxation, a physical sense of well-being. Once the feeling abates, they smoke another cigarette. Pretty soon, one must smoke to maintain that feeling and they are now slaves to smoking. They then will live in slavery until their death, and they might have been "happy" when they smoked all day but they missed out on the freedom they could have had without it. What sin is your cigarette? Is there more potential to this life than our next "fix?"

Those who are in Religious Orders of the Catholic Faith become free of the shackles of the world through their vows. Religious vows help combat this drive to seek the things "below," such as money, power, and sex, and to focus on that which is "above." Vows of poverty, chastity, and obedience are a shield to this chronic pursuit of the lie of happiness.

Now, that does not mean those who look to things above and allow the Holy Spirit to take over their lives cannot have the same feeling that feelings of temporary happiness provide. The fruits of the Holy Spirit are peace and joy. Joy is a Supernatural virtue. Joy is a state of being in the Spirit. Joy is only given to one in relationship with God. To state this differently, *it is impossible for an atheist to have joy.* It is impossible for those living for the things of the world to have joy.

Joy is achieved through the focus of those things "above." It is found through the triumph over sin and addiction. Joy lasts. And by the way, those living for that which is above are not living in a world *mutually exclusive* to "worldly success." That disciple may be materially wealthy, powerful, and have a great physical life in marriage. As long as what one does is always for God's glory and *without attachment*, God will use us all differently with our time here. Remember the rich man – God did not condemn him because he had wealth. The problem came when that wealth was a barrier between the rich man and God and when the attachment to the money itself destroyed the Holy Spirit within him. One cannot serve 2 Masters.

Those who have joy in their lives can experience worldly happiness, *but they do not live for it.* Their joy is maintained even without temporary happiness. That is the secret to all of the saints, especially in their time of suffering. Just read St. Paul. Most of the New Testament was written while he was physically suffering in prison. One cannot help but feel his joy through his writing. He never writes, "Woe is me!!" He is always looking above.

Peace is having a clear conscience. There is no happiness hangover. One in peace can look at God in the eye in love, and without distraction knowing that God has died for their sins. They know that they have forgiven everyone in their lives, and are therefore forgiven themselves. What is blasphemy of the Holy Spirit? (MT 12:30-32) It is the one "unforgivable sin" described by Christ in scripture. **The Holy Spirit is God's mercy.**

When we tamp down the Holy Spirit in our lives, especially in regards to unforgiveness, we are killing the infinite mercy available to us through the blood of the cross.

When we are setting the Spirit loose in our lives, He will compel us to pray. Pray, pray, pray. We can't help it. We talk to Him waking up and going to bed and all day in between. We pray rote prayers, spontaneous prayers, and we will often find ourselves praying with others. We just want to be with Him. We just want to be in His presence. Prayer does not always require words. Sometimes meditation about God brings us into a deeper relationship with Him. Most often, simple gratitude and praise is the greatest prayer. God is found in the silence.

When we are growing in wisdom, we are far more easily taught by God in prayer and through spiritual reading. We can sense what is true more easily in our thoughts, and the thoughts of others. If you seek God in this state, the Holy Spirit is more easily able to consistently break down the lies and snares that the evil one puts in front of us and the confusion he puts in our minds. There becomes a recognition of the Truth more than a learning of it. It is like dejavu. This is the time to read the writings of the saints, the Catechism, and most importantly to read Scripture.

Growing up, I had a significant difficulty reading Scripture. I did not know enough about the construct of the Bible to understand it. I was used to books with a beginning, middle, and an end. It wasn't until college that I learned that the Bible is a library. It is broken down into sections just like a library is broken down into sections. What I found out when the Holy Spirit was uncorked in my life is that I would read the Bible and I wouldn't care so much about the name of this character or that, or even necessarily the sequence of events or details. What really struck me was the point of the story or the event. The Holy Spirit started to make that obvious for me. I was also able to more easily remember these points when speaking to others or applying Scripture to my life.

In our discussion about the Holy Spirit, we must always include the Blessed Mother. She is the spouse of the Holy Spirit. She has no veil between her and God as she was conceived without sin in the Immaculate Conception which prepared her to perfectly carry God within her. She can see perfectly. Even in our weakness, does anybody know you better than your spouse? Does anybody know our God better than His spouse? Mary knows the Master. She is in love with the Holy Spirit. **She experienced the first Pentecost during the incarnation as she was overshadowed with the Holy Spirit as the Word became flesh.** *She is the perfect example of the Holy Spirit set loose* **– all through her humility. All through "Thy will be done." All through "Do whatever He tells you."**

If you want to get to know the Holy Spirit, get to know Mary. Listen to her joy and wisdom in the Magnificat (Lk 1:44-66). Read and listen to her words of knowledge and wisdom. She was thought to be about the age of 14 when she became pregnant with Jesus. I work with tens of thousands of teens. I have never heard them talk like her! Learn to serve her through a consecration to Jesus through her and she will speed up and intensify how much the Holy Spirit can be set loose in your life. I serve her as a captain in this war for souls. If you serve her, she will call you to task, and the ultimate fulfillment of this time here. She will bring you by hand to her Son and will teach you how to love the Holy Spirit more perfectly.

As the Holy Spirit is the action of God, one cannot be "on fire" in the Spirit and lollygag in inaction. The Holy spirit *compels* us to act – It compels us to push ourselves into discomfort. A wise priest once said during Lent, "If it does not hurt, you are doing it wrong." I am telling you now, if you are comfortable in your Faith, there is a problem. You are doing it wrong! The Fire of the Holy Spirit burns our flesh, burns into our lives, and in our humility, burns away our very selves in order for us to become more like our Lord. IT HURTS!!!

The trick with the trial of the deserts in our lives, *and the pain of allowing the Holy Spirit to kill us in our internal crucifixion* is to keep our eyes fixed on Christ above with the resurrection. We must not dwell on this time of testing and trial on this earth which is required for our rebirth in the Spirit. This is the day of a spiritual Confirmation – Our Pentecost. As the first day when our first decision to Follow Christ and to step foot onto the path of life is in a sense our Spiritual Baptism, the days when we pass our test in suffering is our Spiritual Confirmation. This is truly when the "born again" process is complete and you are now an adult apostle of Jesus Christ.

In this mentality, I am willing to wager that the Apostles themselves, despite being in the presence of our Lord Jesus for years and having received the sacraments of Baptism, First Communion, Holy Orders, and Confession, were not Confirmed until Pentecost, becoming adults in our Catholic Faith. Otherwise, they would not have had fear during the crucifixion and they would have died on Christ's left and His right. Only after they were Confirmed in Pentecost was the fruit of the Holy Spirit of courage brought to the surface and set loose. They were able to think, speak, and act in the Spirit, "praying unceasingly." Only after Pentecost, were they free.

Have you experienced your Pentecost yet? Have you experienced your desert? Are you through your desert? If not, seek Our Lady's intercession. Cling to the cross. Trust in God completely. Cut the crap and stop making excuses for your sins. Get rid of all of it. Go to confession today and be done. Do not go back to sin. It is a decision. Trust in God and do not go back this time.

And finally, *after we allow the Holy Spirit to crucify us* by allowing it to destroy our will and our ego, we are then most like the Son of God. Then we can truly be a part of the Trinity for eternity. We are the adopted children of God the Father. His breath runs through all of us. Christ, the first true Son, the Son begotten, not made, is who we are called to be in relationship with the Father. When we die, we will become like Him and partake in the Trinity allowing the infinite power of the Holy Spirit to truly set forth and not only recognize itself in the Father, but *infuse us* into relationship with God the Father for eternity.

Are you ready to say yes to the Holy Spirit in your life? Are you ready to give up control? Are you ready for the crazy adventure that awaits you? Are you ready to die, but then truly live? It is time. There are no accidents. You are here right now and God is giving each one of us a choice. Will you set the Holy Spirit loose in your life? Decide.

Suffering

Confidence. Joy. Hope. Calmness of mind and heart. Wisdom during the storms of life. Fearlessness. PEACE! How does one experience peace of the Holy Spirit in a hostile world where we can often experience suffering?

Most people think of suffering as physical. Physical suffering is often the lowest form. Suffering can be experienced mentally with obsessive thoughts, same sex attraction, gender confusion, thoughts of self-harm, and eating disorders. People can experience emotional suffering through depression, anxiety, or loneliness. There is spiritual suffering with addiction, lack of forgiveness, violence or revenge, low self-esteem, or feelings of not being "worthy of God's love." Most of these types of spiritual suffering have a demonic influence. The torment of demons often attacks the mind and the will. They are like a swarm of gnats in one's mind.

Satan, "the accuser," operates in time. He has us focus on the past where he activates guilt. He also operates in the future, where he gives us anxiety. God acts in the present.

Much of our suffering is the result of free will. Can God love us without having given us a free will? Our sin causes suffering. The sins of others cause suffering. We don't sin in a vacuum. These sins cause deep wounds in others. *Most often those closest to us cause the deepest wounds.* This is often seen with the lack of parents or abusive parents or mentors, having disrespectful or troubled children, adultery in marriage, addiction in families, or betrayal by those we trust. At times, we experience anger at God as the result of loss.

In reality, we are all going to suffer at some point. As much as we try to avoid it, cover it up, or fear it, we will all suffer.

So now what? We can't escape suffering, so how do we deal with it? The early Martyrs give us an example of how to respond to suffering.

The Legend of St. James was that like all of the Apostles after Pentecost; St. James was absolutely fearless. During his trial resulting in his death sentence, St. James was such an effective teacher that a Roman Captain heard his preaching and witnessed his fearlessness as St. James was on his way to be beheaded. Upon the death of St. James, the Roman Captain declared his Christianity on the spot and was beheaded next to St. James. The point of this story is that, like many of the martyrs of the Catholic Faith, St. James had so much peace in the face of adversity and death that his peace and fearlessness was contagious. That is the reason why so many converted to Christianity during those first centuries of martyrdom. Otherwise, who would willingly join those being tortured throughout the Roman Empire? Christians were publicly crucified, fed to lions, enslaved, flogged to death, beheaded, and burned alive. Yet their numbers continued to grow and grow. Their peace and joy *was* the answer to this paradigm.

How did the martyrs come to experience this state of peace and fearlessness? They were able to die to themselves. They died to their EGO. They died to their will and allowed the Holy Spirit to flood unhindered within them. Jesus, when talking to Nicodemus said **we need to be born again.** (Jn 1:21) In the Spirit, which is Peace, once we give everything to the Master and become *like a child* in Faith, totally dedicated to that which is ABOVE, totally dedicated to the mission of attaining Heaven, what do we have to lose? *Freedom is a result of this mentality.* The ability to function as you are destined as a son or daughter of God.

In regards to our hostile world, the world in which we live and where Satan reigns for now, in our Valley of Tears we have our test. Moment to moment we must use our will to choose Heaven, to choose everything above rather than everything we experience below. This test is most often brought on by some sort of suffering.

Romans 8:5 - For those who live according to the flesh are concerned with the things of the flesh, but those who live according to the Spirit, with the things of the Spirit. **The concern of the flesh is death, but the concern of the Spirit is life and peace...**For if you live according to the flesh, you will die, but if by the Spirit, you put to death the deeds of the body, you will live.

We have been taught in Sunday school the New Testament mentality of love and peace and access to God as our Father; however, we often forget that **the door to this resurrection with Him rests *through the crosses of our lives.***

We must get to a deep Truth. In this Valley of Tears, in this place below, God *uses* suffering. **WE MUST GET OUT OF OUR HEADS THAT SUFFERING IS BAD AND PLEASURE IS GOOD.** *All virtue* **is found through suffering.** Fortitude. Patience. Wisdom. Kindness. Self-control. Prudence. Humility. Mercy. Charity. Love.

Look throughout the entire Old Testament. Every time the Israelites would enter the promised land and become comfortable and live for pleasure, God's people would become soft and start to worship idols and intermarry. They would abandon their relationship with God, "Becoming gods unto themselves." They would dive into things of the world, "here below," to chase "happiness" by satisfying all of their senses, rather than pursuing those "things above" - peace and joy. God would then allow the destruction of his chosen people through battles and exile them to the desert or foreign lands, only to have them become so uncomfortable that they would look to Him. We have a God of consolation and desolation.

Now here is the truth about suffering: God allows it for our sanctification. Satan cannot act without God's permission.

2 Corinthians 12 : Therefore, that I might not become too elated, a thorn in the flesh was given to me, and angel of Satan, to beat me, to keep me from being too elated. Three times I begged the Lord about this, that it might leave me, but He said to me, "**My grace is sufficient for you,** *for power is made perfect in weakness.*"…For when I am weak, *then* I am strong.

Why? Because in our weakness, in our desert, when there is only Satan, where you do not feel the presence of the Lord and you feel most alone, where there is no end in sight, where the only whisper you hear is from the evil one who tells you that you just need to kneel to him and all the pleasure in the world will be yours….where the desert sand blows you around until you fall on your face at the Foot of the Cross, holding your only point of reference beneath the Crucified Master, while the sandstorm rips through the air like a tornado, ripping all that you are, breaking you down to dust, to the point where you become *desperately desperate.* Only then, in that lowest moment, with your steadfast holding onto that cross, will you feel the quiet dripping of the Lord's blood on your back, healing you, renewing you, making

you a new creature of pure Faith, honing you like a sword in a furnace. *For in your Death, you become more and more like Him in life.*

That, my friends, is the moment of spiritual warfare. That is the moment between life and death. After suffering occurs, what is your disposition? That is the moment when Satan is most involved. Do you whine and complain? Does suffering cause you to curse God, become skeptical, to become suspicious or are you "already dead" to yourself? Do you instead allow the suffering to draw you closer to Him and to draw all those around you closer to Him? That is where spiritual warfare arises. The battle of the eternal soul. There is only one commodity in the universe.... The soul. Does yours *rest* in Him?

Now how do we fight this battle practically, especially with those who don't yet know Him? How do we help those who are not seeking those things above and are only focusing on that which is below? How do we help those who don't have meaning to their lives? **We can best teach others by the Peace we have in the storms of life.**

To live in peace, to live in the Holy Spirit is not a moment...IT IS A STATE OF BEING. It is to carry on with a child-like faith in God, to Trust Him above all else, regardless of the circumstances. The following is an excerpt from a book my father wrote – Urgent Advice from your Catholic Grandpa.

There was a wise farmer who lived in a small village. His neighbors considered him rich because he owned a horse. The horse did his field work for him. Then one day the horse disappeared. His neighbors gathered around and said, "It is a terrible thing that your horse disappeared." The farmer responded, "It could be good, it could be bad. Who knows?"

Several days later, the farmer's horse reappeared and brought with him several other horses, one for each family in the small village. The villagers again addressed the farmer, "This is fantastic!" The farmer responded, "It could be good, it could be bad. Who knows?"

The farmer then proceeded to train his horse and taught his 18-year-old son to ride it. The son happened to fall off the horse and break his leg. The villagers said to the farmer, "This is very bad. Aren't you upset with the turn of events? What are you going to do?" Again, the famer responded, "It could be good, it could be bad. Who knows?"

A week later, the army came through town and forced every young able-bodied man to join them and go off to war. The army could not take the farmer's son because he had the broken leg. The villagers observed the situation and congratulated the farmer, "Wow!" you must be really happy with what happened." The farmer responded with peace in his voice, "It could be good, it could be bad. Who knows?"

My point is, for those who trust in the Lord, we realize that the Master does not draw in straight lines. He scribbles like a 2-year-old, but things will always work out for those who stay with Him. **I would be willing to assert that everything that happens in our lives is Good for those who love the Lord.**

Peace and Pain can exist at the same time. It is very likely the norm.

When it comes to whether God or Satan is in control of our misery – for those who TRUST in God, who cares? Just know that God is there always to comfort, to purify, *and to give you exactly what it will take for you to return back to him,* **because He loves you!** God Himself knows exactly what you are going through. He was one of us. He endured all the suffering this world has to offer, including the desert. He did not even stop His beloved Son from being crucified. We must pick up our cross and follow Him, all the way to the Resurrection!

Not Alone

Now that does not mean that we have to carry our cross of suffering alone. One day I had an older couple in my office. In conversation, I quickly became aware that the woman had Alzheimer's disease. Her husband cared for her, loved her, and protected her. She didn't even know his name. "In sickness and in health…" This man's oath, his covenant to his wife meant something. He was a genuine hero.

Later I asked the Lord, "Why do you allow Alzheimer's to exist? In essence the meaning of her life, the moment in time here on Earth for her to make the choice for God is over. Why would you continue to allow her to live?"

Shortly after I asked the question, I was listening to Fr. Spitzer, President of Gonzaga University, speaking on EWTN. The answer came through him in the form of the following story I will summarize for you here:

One day, 80 people were invited to a banquet. As they sat there, taking in the wonderful sights and aromas of their favorite food, they attempted to eat. Upon doing so, they discovered they were built without wrists and elbows. This realization caused wailing and gnashing of teeth as they were within inches of their favorite food, yet they could not feed themselves.

The first 20 people surmised, 'There must not be a God, because if there was, He would have built us with wrists and elbows.'

The second group of 20 replied, 'Well, the table is here, we are here, and we are not God, so He must exist. However, He must not be all powerful because if He was, He certainly would have made us with wrists and elbows.'

The third group of 20 stated 'God being God, He would be omnipotent; He would be all powerful. Therefore, He must not be a loving God if He created us without wrists and elbows.'

The fourth group of 20 looked at the others at the table in dismay, *picked up their plates and leaned over the table to feed those across from themselves.*

This fourth group of 20 realized they were built without wrists and elbows *on purpose.* They found they could never truly understand unconditional love if they only fed themselves. In giving of themselves, in serving others, in carrying their cross, only then could they experience sacrificial love, the deepest kind of love.

God allows Alzheimer's not for the spiritual benefit of the individual who has the disease. He allows the situation to exist to give the rest of us the chance to "feed her." In serving her, we receive grace and virtue, virtue that would otherwise be very difficult to obtain, virtue consisting of humility, patience, fortitude, compassion, wisdom, hope, and understanding. Serving her puts each person who encounters her into a spiritual 'boot camp' of sorts, molding the caregiver's soul and preparing it for eternal life with God. The woman's Alzheimer's may very well have saved her husband's soul and was therefore an eternal gift to him from God.

We will all suffer. Most of us will be cognitive through it. We will be acutely aware of our pain. This means that we will all have our chance to be like Jesus and carry a cross. He did not state, "I am carrying this cross so you don't have to carry one." Rather, Jesus challenges us to "Pick up *your* cross and follow me!" (Mt16:24) We will all have the chance to gain virtue through our suffering. Through suffering, we have the opportunity to be like Christ in all ways as we can offer our suffering to God for grace and intercession for others, including the souls of purgatory. We will all experience *humility* in allowing others to care for us.

It is interesting how we were created. We are born into the world as infants, totally dependent on others to care for us. We depend on our parents to feed us, clothe us, change our diapers, and keep us safe. We then grow into adults and often forget that "There is a God and I am not Him." We think we are God and mistakenly think we can control everything. We live life in utter pride. We then get older and our minds and bodies start falling apart. As we start losing our ability to move, hear, see, remember, eat, breathe, and ultimately wipe our own behind, we begin to quickly realize maybe we weren't God all along. Just maybe He was carrying us this whole time! It is during this end of life phase many people find God for the first time as they experience humility.

That is why euthanasia is so abhorred by the Church. It is through the crosses we all experience at the end of our lives and the associated growth of virtue that we, and those around us, inevitably grow spiritually. Many of us are then able to join God in Heaven. In many ways, we can suffer purgatory here on Earth. We can undergo this spiritual cleansing through our physical suffering. I am not saying we need to have a tug of war with God and stay alive at all costs. If someone has a terminal illness, there is nothing wrong with allowing nature to take its course. John Paul II did not choose to go back onto the ventilator at the end of his time here on Earth. Rather, he chose to die as naturally as possible and continued on his journey to join God.

The important issue I am addressing is the purposeful, intentional killing of someone, to "end their suffering." This includes intentionally injecting the infirmed with lethal drugs. This killing includes the failure to maintain basic life support, such as food and water. All *healthy* people will die without food and water. Cases in which feeding tubes are removed *and* sources of nutrition are withheld are murder (for example, the Terri Shiavo case where a woman became mentally handicapped following a cardiac arrest. She had a supportive family that wanted to care for her, yet her husband intentionally starved his wife to death as he felt she would rather be dead than be handicapped).

We must instead serve those who are suffering. As the women served Christ on his journey with the cross, we are all called to comfort and serve each other when we are carrying our crosses. As in the case of the husband growing in virtue for taking care of his wife with Alzheimer's, we too can grow in virtue when we serve one another. However, this does not mean that I have to *like* suffering; this does not mean I have to enjoy serving those who are suffering; this does not mean that I look for suffering; this does not mean that I do not fear suffering.

The good news is that I am in good company. Even Christ, during the agony in the garden the night before His death, said to God the Father, "Take this cup from me."(Mt 26:39) Like Christ, when I am suffering, I frequently ask the Father to ease my pain. Like Jesus, I also then pray that I have the strength and courage to state, "Thy will, not mine, be done."

As a Catholic, I have found that the journey with Christ to the resurrection and eternal bliss must first include a journey with the cross. Being Catholic does not make me immune from suffering. If anything, the Lord is making me more and more aware of those who need to be fed and has called me to serve more and more people that I would have formerly overlooked as I am so frequently wrapped up in myself and my own needs.

If I know that I can use my crosses in life as Christ used His—to grow in virtue for myself and grace for all mankind—then even in suffering I can still experience peace and joy. I remind myself that there are no such things as accidents. I have a choice at the moment of suffering: to wail and gnash my teeth, or to offer it up like Jesus did for mercy and grace.

Now, let's consider healing. Personally, as a Knight of Malta (who have been in existence for 1000 years, and is the oldest lay religious order in the Catholic Church), we take oaths to serve the "Sick and the Poor" and to "Defend the Holy Roman Catholic Church against the enemies of Religion." Part of our ministry with the sick is to serve them for a week in Lourdes France, one of the recognized Catholic visionary sites of the Blessed Mother. Over the past 150 years, thousands of people have been legitimately physically healed by entering the "baths" of Lourdes. While there, a Cardinal asked me the following question on a radio program: "Why bother going to Lourdes? The Lord is present in the Eucharist in every Church at home? Why make the trip across the world to come here to be with Him?"

My response was, "God loves those who go out of their way to spend time with Him in pilgrimage and there is special grace given to those who make the effort. Look at Zacchaeus who climbed a tree to see Our Lord (Lk 19) or the woman who pushed through a crowd to touch His cloak." (MT 9:18-26)

I also explained, "What is the single thing in common with every human being Jesus Christ physically healed during his ministry 2000 years ago in order to prove who He was? The paralytic, the blind man, the deaf, the lepers, even those that Jesus rose from the dead – the little girl and Lazarus?.......They are ALL DEAD TODAY..... Lazarus was raised from the dead only to eventually die later"

We can all pray for grandma or our child or our neighbor to get physically healed from whatever illness they have and they all may be healed physically ..... for a while...but ultimately they will die. Whether we are young or old, death is certain for us all. So then, why were they physically healed? What healing really matters?

"Some men came carrying a paralyzed man but could not get inside, so they made an opening in the roof above Jesus and then lowered the man down. When Jesus saw their faith, he said to the paralyzed man, 'Son, *your sins are forgiven.*'

Some of the teachers of the law interpreted this as blasphemy, since God alone can forgive sins. Jesus said to them, "Why are you thinking these things? Which is easier: to say to the paralytic, 'Your sins are forgiven,' or to say, 'Get up, take your mat and walk?' But that you may know that the Son of Man has authority on earth to forgive sins...He said to the man... Get up, take your mat and go home." (Mk 2: 1-12)

God physically heals for Faith. There is no other reason than to tell you He is there. **Real, lasting and eternal healing happens both in the Confessional where sins are forgiven and upon the reception of the Eucharist.**

Perhaps He will not physically heal you or your loved one if you have enough faith to believe in Him without it. That is why some at Lourdes are physically healed and others are not. If you are reading this book and are bitter because you do not believe that God heard your prayer in your time of need.... *He did.* He always answers prayer – Yes, No, or Not Yet. It is *your* test. He knows that you have been given enough grace to believe in Him without that miracle of physical healing. Will you pass your test? Are you willing to give Him control? Even to the death of those you love? God the Father passed the same test with His only beloved Son.....

What now? Decide suffering is "not bad" and use it as an opportunity. Offer up your crosses. Let go of your past. Let go of those wounds. Forgive others, even if they are evil. Receive the sacraments. Go to confession. Forgive those who have wounded you and choose to love them. *Start thanking God for your Crosses*.....What?!!! Yes.

If you are not suffering, hunt for others that are and become like Simon of Cyrene, the man that was taken into service from the crowd when Christ was carrying His cross.

I often ask myself, "Would I run away from Christ as He was carrying His cross? Would I run from His filthy body as he was covered in blood and dust from repeatedly falling on His journey to His crucifixion? Would I run away from the terror of blood and death? Would I be able to look upon his beaten face, bruised and covered in blood from His crown of thorns? Would I be willing to interrupt my day and daily routine to help Christ with His cross on that journey?"

If I remember to look at all those who suffer as Him, I receive the grace I need to dive into the trenches of life. I become who we are all called to be as true Brothers and Sisters in Christ. **We will never be closer to God than in the moments of carrying His Cross with Him in others!!**

"Now if we are children, then we are heirs—heirs of God and co-heirs with Christ, if indeed we share in his sufferings in order that we may also share in his glory." (Romans 8:17)

Become *desperately desperate* for God, His presence in your life and His Mercy. Know that you have a Father in Heaven rooting for you. All the saints and angels are rooting for you. Your Mother is praying for you and rooting for you. Have the hope of a child. Have the Faith of a child. Have the love of a child! Know that especially in your suffering and service towards others, God loves you!

You must understand that with the Cross comes the Resurrection!!!! Eternal paradise. *We cannot get to Heaven without our crosses.* If I were to tell you that you would receive Heaven through your suffering, would you embrace it? I challenge you to do so, and to use those sufferings to drag as many people with you to the Gates of Heaven as you can; to become the saint you are destined to be.

The Church

Authority. In the realm of religion, authority is everything. Every person and every religious institution has an *opinion* about Truth; the major differentiating factor between them all is *authority*. It would be helpful to retrace our steps a bit and recall how we arrived at this point. Again, we have logically established that God exists. If He exists, there is obviously reason behind Creation. He has given us clues to this reason: like the capacity to have children so we can understand His motives better. He gave us one thing to call our own—a free will—to choose where we go for eternity. He Himself came to earth as Jesus Christ to reveal to us, through example, the way to make the "perfect" choice. If you have followed this journey of logic, and accept it, then welcome to Christianity!

In this day and age, "being a Christian" is a very broad statement. This generally means that either you belong to the Catholic Church, or to one of 33,000 Protestant churches. In my walk with the Lord, I had to carefully consider which of these paths is most consistent with the Truth espoused by Christ.

I decided that to belong to one of these churches, I needed to have faith in the *authority* of that church to teach the Truth. I asked myself, "If Christ is the Son of God, the Messiah, God Himself, would He have become man, revealed to us the perfect example of Truth, died on a cross, only to ascend to Heaven without leaving any *authority* behind to safeguard that perfect standard of Truth throughout time?" What would have been the point of Christ if, after His ascension into Heaven, that perfect standard of Truth just left the Earth? If Christ did not leave any authority, we can imagine that much of His mission would have been in vain.

The reality is that Jesus did leave an authority. In Mathew 16:15, Christ established the first pope.

> "He (Jesus) said to them, "But who do you say that I am?" Simon Peter said in reply, "You are the Messiah, the Son of the living God." Jesus said to him in reply, "Blessed are you, Simon son of Jonah. For flesh and blood has not revealed this to you, but my heavenly Father. And so I say to you, you are Peter, and upon this rock I will build my church, and the gates of the netherworld shall not prevail against it. I will give you the keys to the Kingdom of Heaven. Whatever you bind on earth shall be bound in heaven; and whatever you loose on earth shall be loosed in heaven."

It was Peter, filled with the Holy Spirit after Pentecost, who delivered a lengthy speech to the gathered crowd, spreading the Truth of Christ throughout the world. The entire early church, including St. Paul and all the Apostles, repeatedly deferred to the *authority* of Peter. One example of this was at the first council of the church, the Council of Jerusalem:

> But some from the party of the Pharisees who had become believers stood up and said, "It is necessary to circumcise them (the Gentiles) and direct them to observe the Mosaic Law." The apostles and the presbyters met together to see about this matter. After much debate had taken place, *Peter got up and said to them*, "My brothers, you are well aware that from early days God made his choice among you that through my mouth the Gentiles would hear the word of the gospel and believe. And God, who knows the heart bore witness by granting them the Holy Spirit just as he did us. He made no distinction between us and them, for by faith he purified their hearts. Why, then, are you now putting God to the test by placing on the shoulders of the disciples a yoke that neither our ancestors nor we have been able to bear? On the contrary, we believe that

we are saved through the grace of the Lord Jesus, in the same way as they. The whole assembly *fell silent,* and they listened while Paul and Barnabas described the signs and wonders God had worked among the Gentiles through them." Acts 15: 5-12.

As this passage from the Acts of the Apostles demonstrates, there was much debate, but then *Peter spoke* and the debate about allowing gentiles to directly become Catholic without first becoming Jewish was immediately settled. Within the Catholic Church, since Jesus himself gave Peter the "keys to Heaven and Earth," there has been an authority that has remained throughout history; we call that authority "the pope." The person who presently "sits in Peter's chair" for the church is Pope Francis. The Catholic bishops are the present-day apostles. These bishops have an apostolic lineage of authority that has been passed down through the generations from Peter and the first apostles till now. This lineage is known as Apostolic Succession. **If you believe God is Truth and became incarnate in the person of Jesus Christ, then you should believe in the "fullness of Truth" that has been safeguarded by the Catholic Church for the past 2000 years as Christ himself established the Catholic Church through Peter.**

There have been several councils of the Church over the past 2000 years. All these councils have been similar to that first Council of Jerusalem. There is normally a topic of faith which requires debate and clarification but, in the end, when statements are made by the bishops in union with the pope, a Catholic can have faith in the Truth set forth by these councils. In the teaching of faith and morals, *there are always consistent teachings.* We can have faith in the Church because of the Church's authority. ***Without authority,* there is only opinion.**

The Catholic Church has three "pillars of faith." A pillar of faith is used to reveal the fullness of the Truth on Earth. All three pillars of faith work in unison and are never contradictory. The first pillar of faith is the Tradition of the Church. This Tradition is the collection of teachings and customs passed from generation to generation to maintain the words and actions of Jesus—to maintain the Truth. This Tradition was maintained through oral history for years and also existed *before* the gospels were written and the Bible and New Testament were constructed. This Tradition includes all the divine revelation captured and collected so that every generation of Catholics doesn't have to "reinvent the wheel." There is a significant advantage to having the ability to theologically stand on the shoulders of giants.

The second pillar of faith is the Magisterium of the Church. This is the teaching authority discussed above which includes the bishops in union with the pope. The members of this group are the shepherds Christ put in charge to guide His Church till the end of time. The Magesterium existed *before* the Gospels and the entire New Testament was constructed. The Magesterium preserves, teaches, and hands on the "Deposit of Faith," the Tradition of the Church while having the authority to interpret Scripture.

Finally, the third pillar of faith is Scripture itself. The Catholic Church believes the Bible is divinely inspired. As Christ recognized the authority of Scripture, so do Catholics.

It is through the combination and union of these "pillars of faith" that the Catholic Church boldly claims to have the "Fullness of the Truth." This is not to say that other religions do not contain some Truth. However, some of these religions contain more Truth than others. But the Truth found in these faiths is ultimately the Truth already recognized by the Catholic Church. **In the realm of faith and morals, the Catholic Church lacks nothing as the Catholic Church is the Church of Jesus Christ who lacks nothing.**

Our Protestant brothers and sisters also have a significant amount of Truth in their faith. Many of my closest friends and relatives come from a Protestant background. (Note that I use the word "Protestant" to refer to all Western non-Catholic Christians.) I have truly learned a lot from these brothers and sisters in Christ. I do not doubt their faith or relationship with the Lord. What is funny is that most of these non-Catholic Christians don't really know what our differences are. Too many times I have missed an opportunity to truly question why we Christians are still divided. Do we not all believe in a Lord of unity? Do we not believe that God desires a unified "Body of Christ?" As I draw closer to the Lord, I often feel that He probably 'rolls his eyes' at our petty squabbles about practically nothing. **Division is never from God.** It is hard to submit to an authority bigger than one's own interpretation of Truth.

could offer us, the sheep, more of their attention. *They have died unto themselves for you and me.*

Being a priest in this age is extremely difficult. Imagine serving a parish that used to take 4-6 priests to manage. Imagine living life, practically alone. Since the recent scandal, they cannot even be adopted by a parish family without suspicion. During this time when we are short of priests, entering parish life is like signing up to go onto an island, since it is so much logistically harder to experience fraternity with their peers. It reminds me of a movie called "Cast Away" (2000) with Tom Hanks. In the movie, a very rational, normal guy gets shipwrecked on an island. After a time, he is so lonely that he starts talking to a volleyball that washes up on shore that he names 'Wilson.'

I have at times had *rare* interactions with certain priests and found that some are a bit socially awkward. Yep, some of these men are talking to 'Wilson.' Then I think about the simple reality that these men have died to themselves. They knowingly chose to go to that island with their 'yes' and have answered the call of the Lord. It is much like the Annunciation when Mary said 'yes' to the Archangel Gabriel. **Through her 'yes,' God became incarnate into flesh as Jesus Christ. Through our priest's same 'yes,' God becomes incarnate into flesh as the Eucharist.** It is through this latter realization that my heart has been opened to total compassion and respect for these men. I love all of these guys, even the ones talking to 'Wilson.' How often I take for granted their presence in my life. How often I have missed the opportunity to thank them for their sacrifice. We all need to invite our priests into our community again. We all need to offer respite from their lonely island. Priests are heroes that have been on the front lines for souls for many years…. Under chronic and persistent attack from Satan. The perpetual fight for souls takes its toll! Gratitude, respect, compassion, understanding, love and support. That is what we owe these Heroes!

Tangents, Ryan, tangents! Back to our Protestant brethren. The fundamental problem with Martin Luther rejecting the Church was that, instead of focusing specifically on the abuses he saw with the practical management of the Church, he started to change his core beliefs in the realm of faith and morals to his own liking. His new religion was so uniquely his own, it ultimately came to be called the Luther-an church.

He eliminated the first two "pillars of faith" all together and he, like the 33,000 other protestant denominations, believe in only one pillar of faith: that of Scripture alone.

What Luther failed to recognize is that oral tradition came *before* scripture. It was only after the Apostles recognized that the Second Coming of Christ was not likely to occur in their lifetime that the gospels were finally written down, thirty to fifty years after the death of Christ! It was the Catholic Church that decided during the Council of Hippo (393AD) and Carthage (397AD) which books of the Bible were "divinely inspired" and therefore included.

By eliminating the belief in any authority and using Scripture alone, Martin Luther set up a system inclined to perpetuate continuous division because *people interpret scripture differently*. Without a Magisterium to provide an interpretation of scripture consistent with tradition, a Protestant church may be in a situation where it thrives only as long as its pastor is present. The moment that pastor leaves, or there is a disagreement or debate about the interpretation of scripture within that church because there is no authority or tradition, there is a risk that the church will break down into more protestant sects. That is one significant reason that there are currently over 33,000 different Protestant denominations in the United States. Even within the Lutheran faith, one Lutheran service may be different from another Lutheran service that takes place down the street because again, the entire Protestant faith is based primarily upon the interpretation of scripture by the individual pastor. The Bible was and is a source of Truth. However, without the context of tradition since the time of Christ, and without the shepherds in the Magisterium to guide the flock, the sheep will interpret scripture as they see fit. The Truth is then dependent upon the views of the individual pastor or some kind of democratic process such as a group of "elders."

The reason why many Protestant churches seem to be "on fire with the Spirit" is because most of these churches are first- or second-generation churches. Most of the people in the church have freely chosen to be there for a specific reason. The question about the teaching message given in a church—beyond all the bells and whistles—is what the church looks like after four or five generations when the members have not freely chosen to join the church on their own accord but were born into the faith. Churches struggle to stand the test of time when the initial zeal has died along with its original members.

Taking a step back and looking into this objectively, do you really think that the Truth of the universe is based on each of our whim? Would Christ have intended on leaving a church with these continuous divisions? Would Christ have left us without a Shepherd? Would He have expected us to individually come to the Truth ourselves without taking into consideration the Truths found by our forefathers? Do we believe we are really the first ones to come up with questions about our faith? Do we believe that no one else throughout Christian history has come up with any answers? **Was Jesus wrong when He stated that "the netherworld will not prevail against it (the Catholic Church under Peter's authority)?"**

At the end of the day, I believe a lot of protestant Christians frequently *act* upon the "Truths" established by the Catholic Church better than some Catholics, whether the Protestant recognizes this reality or not. In my experience, they have been incredibly supportive in advancing all things in Christ's name. We are all truly brothers and sisters in Christ. If you are a non-Catholic Christian, I implore you to discover the origins of your protestant sect. I ask that you look for the *authority* of your faith. *When* you find that it does not originate historically with Christ Himself, I implore you to consider returning home to the Catholic family. There are so many people that look at us (Christians) as the enemy. Now, more than ever before, we need to stand as one. Lord, grant us the courage to rationally face our differences with a spirit of love in you. Unify us in this time of division. Help us to die to ourselves so we can open our heart to *your* authority. I trust you Lord.

Holy Communion

This chapter discusses the "Source and Summit" of the Catholic Church and is highly detailed and advanced. It is too complicated to understand if you have never been to a Catholic Mass. If you are a Non-Catholic reading this book, skip this chapter. If you are Protestant and curious why Catholics do what they do, read on...

I have learned that God has given us a time machine that brings us back in time to witness first-hand the Last Supper of Jesus Christ and His crucifixion. We can literally eat and drink with Christ and physically stand at the foot of the cross, gazing upon the Savior who is dying for our sins. We can then come into union with Him, becoming *one* with His resurrected body, blood, soul, and divinity. We can also become *one* with the Church family through the same Communion. We can do this today, right now, at any Mass held throughout the world.

When I was growing up, I always looked at the Mass as a *meal* in which the "Body of Christ," the Church, gathers to build community. I believed that the meal shared at church with the 'Church family' was similar to the meal I shared at home with my family. This is, in fact, true. Mealtime is a critically important opportunity to share with one another, to learn about one another, to encourage each other, to learn about our Faith, to strengthen relationships, and to grow more unified as a family. I can tell you that there is no time more precious at home than the meal time I spend with my family. However, what I discovered in college is that, although we draw closer to each other at Mass in relationship, the essence of Mass is much, much deeper and incredibly profound. I had not yet remotely grasped the magnitude of what actually occurs in this Sacrament of Holy Communion.

The Mass has its roots all the way back to the book of Genesis with Abraham. In short, Abraham desperately wanted a son. He was obedient to God and God established a covenant (a contract) with Abraham. As a result of Abraham's obedience, God promised Abraham "descendants as numerous as the stars."(Gen15:5) Ultimately, Isaac was born. Abraham loved "his only beloved son."

As the story continued, Abraham's faith and obedience were put to the test. The Lord asked Abraham to sacrifice "his only beloved son." Genesis 22:1-13

> Sometime after these events, God put Abraham to the test. He called to him, "Abraham!" "Ready!" he replied. Then God said: "Take your son Isaac, your only one, whom you love, and go to the land of Moriah. There you shall offer him up as a holocaust on a height that I will point out to you...Thereupon Abraham *took the wood for the holocaust and laid it on his son Isaac's shoulders,* while he himself carried the fire and the knife. As the two walked on together, Isaac spoke to his father Abraham: "Father!" he said. "Yes, son," he replied. Isaac continued, "Here are the fire and the wood, but where is the lamb for the holocaust?" "Son," Abraham answered, *"God himself will provide the lamb for the holocaust."* Then the two continued forward. When they came to the place of which God told him, Abraham built an altar there and arranged the wood on it. Next he tied up his son Isaac, and put him on top of the wood on the altar. Then he reached out and took the knife to slaughter his son. But the Lord's messenger called to him from heaven, "Abraham, Abraham!" "Yes Lord," he answered. "Do not lay your hand on the boy," said the messenger. "Do not do the least thing to him. I know now how devoted you are to God, since you did not withhold from me your own beloved son." As Abraham looked about, he spied a ram caught by its horns in the thicket. So he went and took the ram and offered it up as a holocaust in place of his son.

This concept of an only beloved son carrying wood on his shoulders to be sacrificed sure sounds a lot like a preview to the crucifixion of Jesus Christ. Considering the reality that Isaac was large enough to carry the wood of the sacrifice on his shoulders and that his father, Abraham, was an old man, Isaac likely offered himself to be bound prior to the sacrifice. The Jews built Solomon's temple on the traditional site of where that event occurred. When the Jews sacrificed the unblemished lambs in the temple, a ram's horn was blown to remind God that "He will provide the lamb (Jesus Christ)." When John the Baptist first saw Jesus, he boldly proclaimed "Behold the Lamb of God that takes away the sins of the world."(Jn1:29)

The Jewish Passover is another example of the tradition of the "sacrifice of the lamb." In Exodus 12:3-8 we find the verse:

> "Tell the whole community of Israel: On the tenth of this month every one of your families must procure a lamb...The lamb must be a year old and without blemish. You may take it from either the sheep or the goats. You shall keep it until the fourteenth day of this month, and then, with the whole assembly of Israel present, it shall be slaughtered during the evening twilight. They shall take some of its blood and apply it to the two doorposts and the lintel of every house in which they partake of the lamb. That same night *they shall eat its roasted flesh with unleavened bread* and bitter herbs."

On Palm Sunday, Christians celebrate Jesus entering Jerusalem. Historically it happened to be the same day that the "unblemished" lambs were likewise being ushered to the temple. At the Passover meal itself the following Thursday evening, Jesus took the unleavened bread "said the blessing, broke it, and giving it to his disciples said, "Take and eat; this is my body." Then he took a cup, gave thanks, and gave it to them, saying, "Drink from it, all of you, for this is my blood of the covenant, which will be shed on behalf of many for the forgiveness of sins." (Mt 26:26-28)

It was at the Passover meal that Christ gave Himself *to be consumed*: body, blood, soul, and divinity just as the Jews would normally consume

In receiving Christ, the Lord gives to me all the grace I am open to, and capable of, receiving.

Many times at Mass, I cringe as many of my fellow churchgoers do not seem to understand what is going on. Through evident lack of reverence, it is clear that there is some confusion with where they are, what they are doing, and WHO they are receiving. As they bolt from the church early to their cars to beat traffic, knocking over old ladies and cursing, I have often asked myself, "is the Eucharist they just received minutes ago broken?!!" Didn't they just receive the tidal wave of grace that God offers in every Eucharist? Didn't many saints literally survive physically on the Eucharist alone? Didn't others go into states of ecstasy? **The proportion of grace I receive in the Eucharist is directly proportional to the amount I have died to myself that can be replaced by Him.** Some receive an ocean of grace, others just a shot glass.

If you have doubt about the true and complete presence of Christ in the Eucharist, you are not alone. If you were to ever memorize a verse from Scripture, the following would be the one to remember. My Protestant friends who seem to have the entire Bible memorized chapter and verse generally leave me alone after we discuss John 6:47-69:

> "Amen, Amen I say to you, whoever believes has eternal life. I am the Bread of Life. Your ancestors ate the manna in the desert and they died; this is the bread that comes down from Heaven so that one may eat it and not die. **I am the Living Bread that came down from Heaven; whoever eats *this* bread will live forever; and the bread that I will give is <u>my flesh</u> for the life of the world."** The Jews quarreled among themselves, saying, "How can this man give us his flesh to eat?" Jesus said to them, "Amen, Amen I say to you, **unless you eat of the flesh of the Son of Man and drink his blood, you do not have life within you. Whoever eats my flesh and drinks my blood has eternal life, and I will raise him on the last day. For my flesh is true food, and my blood is true drink. Whoever eats my flesh and drinks my blood remains in me and I in him.** This is the bread that came

down from Heaven. Unlike your ancestors who ate and still died, whoever eats this bread will live forever." Then many of his disciples who were listening said "This saying is hard; who can accept it?"...As a result of this, many of his disciples returned to their way of life and no longer accompanied Him. Jesus then said to the Twelve, "Do you also want to leave?" Simon Peter answered Him, "Master, to whom shall we go? You have the words of eternal life. We have come to believe and are convinced that you are the Holy One of God."

In Scripture, because there was no ability to have bold print or italics, important points were repeated for emphasis. The prior verse was the single most repeated verse by Christ in the entire gospel. Jesus never said the Eucharist was a *symbol* of anything. He was so specific about this Truth that he was willing to allow all of his followers, including his twelve Apostles to leave him over it. His closest friends, his apostles, didn't understand at the time what the Lord was talking about. Peter (as usual) states, "To whom shall we go?" They had faith *without* understanding.

Jesus Christ is fully present, body blood soul and divinity in the Eucharist, whether or not I believe it. Again, there is nothing less relevant to the Truth and Reality of the universe than my personal opinion. Truth and Reality do not bend to my will, as "There is a God, and I am not Him." **Jesus is fully present in the Eucharist because *He* said so.** It is really that simple.

I have asked myself about this Truth, that is, the true presence of God in this cup of wine or this piece of unleavened bread. In my doubt I ask myself one question, "Where else would I go?" I have accepted the fact that, in this case like many others, I do not know everything or understand everything. I am a spiritual child. I have faith that my Church, my spiritual mother, has my best interests at heart. Like a mother, to the extent I can understand, it is her goal to teach me Truth.

When my children were two years old, I would tell them that the stove was hot. No matter how much the two-year-old would argue about it, or will it to be otherwise, the stove remained hot. My children didn't have to believe it, or understand it to be true, in order for the hotness of the stove to be reality. Ultimately, if they disobeyed me and touched the stove, they got burned.

My spiritual mother, the Church, is the same. Based on her knowledge of Christ and her 2000 years of collective experience and wisdom, the Church has a thorough grasp of the difference between *healthy* spiritual behavior versus *unhealthy* spiritual behavior. Like my worldly mother, the Church remains with me as a support to comfort me if I touch the hot, spiritual stove and get spiritually burned.

I am not recommending that one remain ignorant about *why* the Church teaches what it does. Through asking questions, I can mature in my faith. I can learn to obey not out of fear that the stove is hot. Instead, I can learn to obey *because I love my mother*. This is how a mature relationship with the Lord and His Church can be achieved. But in the end, because of my trust in the intentions of my mother, the Church, I obey with or without understanding. Later, I may be blessed with the "why" of things when the Lord determines the appropriate time to teach me and I am open to hearing the Truth.

Christ is truly present at every Mass, in every country throughout the world, every day. It doesn't matter if the priest is boring, old, young, mean, fantastic, holy, crazy, or even speaks your language. Nothing else matters other than the fact that *Christ Himself* is there. The Angels of Heaven kiss the fingers of your priest as he holds in his hands the body, blood, soul, and divinity of God. These Angels do not discriminate who the priest is because wherever Christ is present; that is all that matters. The specific celebrant of the Mass is irrelevant to me. I go to Mass as often as I possibly can to receive Christ. The Catholic Church believes we should be nourished by the grace of the Eucharist *at least* weekly and on Holy Days. If Heaven is our objective and grace is what will help to get us there, we should consider making it to Mass daily.

The kids in my Confirmation class often comment that Mass is "boring." I would then explain that God didn't put His cross in our presence to entertain us. I don't attend Mass to be entertained. Rather, I attend Mass to be in the *presence of God* when He suffers and dies for my sins. Once the kids understand that the center of the universe, the ground zero of salvation, is based on this sacrifice of the cross present at every Mass; once they understand they are to offer themselves on that same altar; then Mass is no longer viewed as some form of entertainment, but the truest reality.

It is the grace of the Cross, the grace of every Mass, which unites Heaven to Earth. As much as God is present to us all the time, by coming to us body, blood, soul, and divinity through the Eucharist, God is *uniquely present* to us at Mass. Once I understood the Truth about God's real presence at Mass, my behavior changed. There is no earthly priority that can even come close to the priority of being present at the foot of that Cross. Sleep, sports, family events, shopping, work, and school—*nothing* is more important to my salvation than the reception of Christ at Mass. **If what I am doing is not benefiting my journey to salvation, I am wasting my time.** I would be forgetting the meaning of my life.

The Eucharist is the "Source and Summit" of our Catholic Faith because it is Christ Himself! As the Eucharist is the Source and Summit of the Faith, it therefore becomes the Source and Summit of our very lives! It becomes the highest priority.

When I go to meet God, I try to respect Who it is I am about to receive. I fast from food one hour prior to Mass. I try to arrive early and I don't rush out at the end. I genuflect (kneel) toward the tabernacle before entering the pew and when leaving the church. I dress appropriately for Mass in respect for the Lord who has invited me to His house. I try to focus on what is transpiring at Mass, especially during the consecration. In giving of myself completely in sacrifice, I offer to the Lord my voice at Mass and expect my kids, with voices good and bad, to do the same. I kneel throughout the consecration and bow my head respectfully at the consecration itself. I also bow just before receiving Christ in the Eucharist. In trying to be as reverent as I can be, I also now receive Christ directly on the tongue.

Before receiving Christ in the Eucharist, I need to be ready spiritually. If I have mortal sin on my soul, I must first confess that sin in Confession. Otherwise, the act of receiving Christ with mortal sin on my soul is a *sacrilege* (a serious sin caused by the irreverent act).

> "Therefore, whoever eats the bread and drinks the cup of the Lord unworthily will have to answer for the body and blood of the Lord. A person should examine himself, and

so eat the bread and drink the cup. For anyone who eats
and drinks without discerning the body, eats and drinks
judgment on himself. That is why many among you are
ill and infirm, and a considerable number are dying."
(1Cor11:27)

If the Eucharist is just a symbol, why would one need to "be worthy"
prior to receiving it? If I am not prepared to receive Christ, I must still
attend Mass to be with my church family. If I miss Church without being
in the hospital sick or other serious reason, it could be a sin of grave matter
requiring the sacrament of Confession prior to receiving the Lord in the
Eucharist again. The only person keeping me out of grace is myself. God
wants me home. He even wants me home if I am covered in sin. As I
mentioned before, all venial (non-serious) sin can be forgiven upon the
reception of the Eucharist.

The Lord loves to be present fully to His children at the Mass. One
evening my youngest sister (as an adult) decided she was going to sleep late
and miss Mass the following morning. I told her, "The Lord expects you to
be at Mass." She laughed and said, "Prove it." I said, "God will wake you
up and not allow you to fall back asleep." She is a very deep sleeper and
didn't take my comment seriously. The next morning, true to my prophecy,
a large fly buzzed around her room and landed repeatedly on her sleeping
face. It finally bothered her enough that she got up in time for Mass and
decided to attend. She later thanked me for 'kicking her in the butt' and
has attended Mass at least weekly since then.

The time machine God has given to all of us is such a blessing. To be
back in time with Christ at the time of his death we have the opportunity
to truly know Him "through the breaking of the bread." (Lk 24:35)

Mary

Mary. The *most beloved* of God. His special star. His *greatest hope*. His *highest creation*. His joy!

I was introduced to my spiritual mother in the eighth grade. At that time one of my older sisters was the family rebel. She was a typical teenager, depressed and angry at the world. Most of that anger was directed at my parents. She seemed compelled to break every rule my parents made. She was clearly searching for something to fill the void of emptiness when the "success of the world" did not offer the lasting joy she had been promised by the world.

She ultimately read a book about Medjugorje, Yugoslavia, where the Blessed Mother is been believed by many to be appearing to six young children. She felt compelled to travel to Europe, across the entire world in her search for Truth. She found what she was looking for… She found Jesus Christ there in Medjugorje! She had a miraculous experience. When she returned, she was unrecognizable as my sister. Suddenly she had peace in her soul and a purpose to her life. She started to serve others and was no longer depressed and angry. Her change was so radical that my father took note and was dumbfounded. He started to read a lot about our Catholic Faith. Then, as the shepherd of our family, he began his new journey and, together with my mom, brought the rest of us closer to Christ in a personal way. I can assure you that without the experience my sister had in Medjugorje, I would not be writing this book today.

Who is Mary? Mary is a hero! She is a hero's hero. She is "the New Eve," one of God's greatest gifts to His children. She is the New Ark of the Covenant, carrying God within her, the greatest spiritual warrior, the exemplification of humility, the intercessor, the Immaculate Conception, the Queen of Heaven and Earth… She is the Mother of GOD.

Unlike all of us, she participates *perfectly* in the Trinity. She is the daughter of the Father, the spouse of the Holy Spirit, and the Mother of the Son.

As fantastically amazing as Mary is, **she has no power of her own.** Like the moon, she can only shed light on the world by reflecting the Sun/Son. She is always taking her children to Him. She is always there, lighting our path to Him.

What is clear is that Jesus listens to her. He followed the Ten Commandments and "honored his father and mother."(Ex20:12) One example of this was during the wedding feast at Cana. According to John 2:3-6, "When the wine ran short, the mother of Jesus said to him, 'they have no wine.' Jesus said to her, 'Woman, how does your concern affect me? My hour has not yet come.' His mother said to the servers, *'Do whatever He tells you.'*"

This story tells us a lot about the relationship between Christ and the "Woman." First, like God the Father in Genesis ("I will put enmity between you and the Woman"), Christ always refers to his mother throughout scripture as "Woman." Second, Christ obeyed his mother even though his hour "has not yet come," allowing her to intercede for the bride and groom. Finally, she instructed the servants to "do whatever He tells you."

This entire story is a microcosm of Mary's role in the universe. Mary intercedes for us. God simply loves her. While raising nine kids, my mother's instinctual answer to the constant barrage of requests to her throughout a day was 'no.' That instinct of hers usually kept most of us out of trouble. We all knew that if we really wanted something, we could always pass the request through my father. He would *intercede* for us and, at times, the outcome would be quite different.

Mary intercedes for her children like this all of the time. There is no better person one could have whispering into the ear of the Lord than His mother. When Catholics recite the 'Hail Mary,' we are simply asking the Mother of God to intercede for us at the two most important times in our existence, "now and at the hour of our death." It is similar to asking your wife, cousin, mother, or friend to pray for you, like we all do when we are sick or facing challenges. The prayer to ask for the intercession of Mary has a bit more influence with our Lord however. **Our prayers are magnified through her.** *She is a quiet, steady, loving, peaceful presence.*

It would be foolish to "worship" Mary. Why would someone worship a creature other than God, especially if that creature had no power? Catholics do not worship Mary. Catholics *honor* her. If we want to be like Christ in all ways, we must honor His mother. This is especially true because He gave us His mother, His final gift from the cross, before His death.

> "When Jesus saw his mother and the disciple there whom he loved (John), he said to his mother, 'Woman, behold, your son.' Then he said to the disciple, 'Behold, your mother.'" John 19:26-27.

During crucifixion, one would normally die through suffocation rather than by bleeding to death. This occurred because as one would hang on the cross, their arms would be stretched straight over their head and, over time, they would not be able to support their own body weight. In order for Christ to fully breathe, much less speak, He would have to pull on the nails holding His hands and push on the nail through His feet to elevate Himself on the cross in order to inhale enough in order to speak. In other words, it took a lot of effort and pain for Jesus to speak while He was hanging from the cross. It is because of this reality that I pay close attention to the few words of Christ while He was on the cross.

Jesus Himself gave us His mom to be our own. We all have this great mom who wants nothing more than for us to know her Son. She wants nothing more than for us to spend eternity with God and our eternal family in Heaven. I talk to Mary every day. I am a "mama's boy." I have been consecrated to Christ through Mary for years, meaning that I have requested that she magnify all of my prayers to the Son.

Initially, I had a hard time in my relationship with her as I had a hard time imagining her as my Mother. My perception completely changed when in talking to a priest. He said, "that instead of envisioning her as mother, envision her as Queen. Then envision yourself as her Captain and go from there." That worked for me. I consecrated myself to Christ through her by reading *33 days to Morning Glory* (Fr. Michael Gaitley) and she has been present in my life like a shadow ever since. As her Captain, I try to please her by drawing all souls that I possibly can to her Son. In reward, she will be there, "At the hour of my death" to be my advocate *to* the Son.

Jesus is not jealous of my love for her. Why wouldn't I want to know and love the human being closest to Jesus when He walked the earth? It would certainly strain any relationship I would have with one of my friends if I brought him home to my house and he didn't honor, respect, or even want to talk to my mother. Jesus is the same. If I really want to love Christ; if I really want to know everything about Him; if I want to become one with Him; I need to know His mother.

Throughout time, Mary has appeared to visionaries in several places on Earth. In each one of these miraculous appearances, her message always points to her Son saying "Do whatever He tells you." Before you shake your head and question the authenticity of these visions, you should know that the Catholic Church is the most skeptical party before declaring one of these visionary sites to be authentic. The Church launches full investigations which often take decades before declaring a miracle.

Many Catholic pilgrims flock to these sites where visions have occurred. These include Fatima Portugal, Lourdes France, Guadalupe Mexico, and Knock Ireland. The Church has yet to recognize Medjugorje because the visions are still believed by many to be occurring today and the investigation by the Church does not begin until the purported visions have ceased.

Following in the steps of my sister, many others in my family have since visited Medjugorje. Some have returned with more dramatic life changing stories than others. All have returned with a closer relationship to Christ from the experience. In going to Medjugorje, or making any pilgrimage for that matter, God seems to recognize our effort to know Him better. God seems to honor those who are willing to stop for a moment of their life and make a journey to see Him.

For years, I have been the singing cantor at my parish meaning that I sit up front near the altar at every Mass. This is especially hard on my wife who then has to sit in the entrance vestibule of the Church with our numerous super-hyperactive ADD children. Mass is especially difficult for all of them. For years, she would be very concerned about the kids disturbing others who chose to stay in the vestibule, rather than enter the Church. I repeatedly told her not to worry, they can choose to go inside, however she could not.

One day after Mass, I could see her like an Irish storm cloud at 50 yards, red faced and hair curling. "Oh crap," I thought to myself. I made it to the car, allowed the silence to enwrap us both, and after 30 seconds asked quietly, "What happened?"

She relayed, "A very kind, well-meaning woman came up to me at the end of Mass and stated, "Perhaps if you pray to the Blessed Virgin Mary, she can help you with these children."

My wife then looked at me in the eyes. In her perfect, saintly candor and said, "Now I ask you this.... What on earth does the Blessed Mother know about raising *these* children??!!! I am rather certain that Jesus was easier!" I am sure the blessed Mother laughed at this honesty but the description of her scenario is not entirely accurate.

Mary does not have a veil between her and God. Due to her Immaculate Conception, she is not stained by the fall. She can see all evil *as it is*. All sin in her presence is excruciatingly painful to her! Imagine a 2-year-old innocent child watching a horror movie every day and never becoming desensitized. What an attack on her mentally, emotionally, and spiritually. Because of this reality, she understands and *feels* the Cross, not only as Christ's mother, but as the pure, innocent unblemished soul that she is. When I think of Mary at the foot of the cross, I often try to put myself in her shoes. Can you imagine watching *your* child being beaten and tortured in front of you? Can you imagine the love of your life having a crown of thorns banged into his scalp, having nails driven through his hands and feet, and hung up like a criminal? Could you imagine a mother's instinct to simply want to hold her son who is suffering, wipe the blood from his face, and kiss him like she would have when he was a boy to make him feel better? As was foreseen by Simeon at Jesus' circumcision, her heart was truly pierced as she was tortured, sharing her son's pain. (Lk 2:34)

Better than anyone, Mary understands God's sacrifice for us. She is truly an example to all of us. In the end, I speak to Mary as first did the Angel Gabriel and Elizabeth (Mary's Aunt):

"Hail Mary, full of grace, the Lord is with thee. Blessed art thou among women and blessed is the fruit of thy womb, Jesus. Holy Mary, Mother of God, pray for us sinners now, and at the hour of our death. Amen."

Prayer

Relationships are the only things that transcend time and last forever. Relationships are the only things that are not dust. In all relationships, communication is paramount. This is especially true with spouses and children. It most definitely applies to our relationship with God.

Without communication, relationships die. Just ask any divorcee or child who is distant from a parent. I have found that my relationship with God is no different. *Without* prayer, it would be like telling the Lord, "I love you. I will give up everything for you. I just don't want to talk to you, think about you, listen to you, or be around you."

Prayer is simply communication with the Lord. This communication doesn't mean I always need to use words. Sometimes I just sit with my wife. We don't need to talk about anything. We just hold hands and sit together. We are *present* to one another. This communicates to her that she is important to me. This lets her know that there is nothing more important to me at that moment than her. This gives me a moment where I might be more apt to listen.

Similarly, I sometimes just sit with the Lord in what is called Adoration (or Exposition) of the Eucharist. It is like sitting on the porch with my wife. To enable Adoration, a consecrated Communion Host—that is the body, blood, soul, and divinity of Jesus Christ—is placed by the Catholic priest or Deacon in a transparent receptacle called a monstrance. I just sit there in His presence. Sometimes I talk; sometimes I listen. In all cases, being with Him in person is like getting a Son/suntan of grace. There is something special about stopping my life for a moment to simply *be* with the Lord. Like taking a pilgrimage, God seems to appreciate the effort. He rewards my life with peace and joy, no matter how tough things of the world are. Now that doesn't mean I don't have normal anxiety about my worldly responsibilities. In prayer, God simply re-centers my priorities and gives me the grace to endure.

In many ways, my whole life is a prayer. Each morning I offer up my day to the Lord to do with me as He wills. I ask Him to help me to have the courage to die to my will. I offer up the challenges He places before me and I ask for the wisdom to never miss an opportunity to bring others to Him. I live my life with an acute awareness that *there are no accidents*. I ask to become aware of the purpose of the present moment and try to learn from every situation the Lord brings me.

In my journey of life, I often reflect on my day and ask God to identify those areas in me that need the most correction. Prayer is like an x-ray for the soul. I have so many weaknesses. However, with the insight God gives me, I am able to focus my prayer and ask for the grace (spiritual medicine) to address my specific spiritual illness in sin.

Other than the Mass itself, the greatest prayer I have ever encountered is the prayer of the rosary. The rosary is an organized prayer by which I am able to think about various times of Christ's life. The genius of the rosary is that by reciting the "Hail Mary's" and "Our Father's," *it creates a disciplined amount of time* where I am meditating on Christ's life. Through that meditation, I can learn to emulate that perfect example. Beyond that, it is too complicated to describe how to pray the rosary in this book. My advice would be to research how to pray it or ask your priest. It will change your life.

Praying the rosary is a powerful spiritual weapon. Satan hates it. I start praying the rosary at times when I am tempted; there seems to be nothing more effective in refocusing my mind on my master and friend, Jesus Christ. It is a prayer that opens a font of grace in my life.

Let me tell you a secret. I really don't enjoy praying the rosary. It takes a lot of discipline. The rosary is a spiritual *exercise.*

I also don't like physical exercise. There is nothing I like to do less than run on a treadmill. However, I do it because it makes me physically healthy. After I work out, I feel great. I feel physically fast and alert and ready for the physical challenges of that day. If I miss my regular workout, I feel physically slow and dull and out of shape when I am physically challenged that day.

organized prayer is healthy for our relationship. A disciplined prayer life is needed to stay on track.

There is no greater place to experience the combination of both organized and spontaneous prayer than the Mass itself. At any Catholic Church I might attend throughout the world, at any given moment, the essential prayers are consistent at the Mass and the format is essentially the same everywhere. It is truly the "Mystical Body of Christ" speaking and praying in one voice to the Father, "Remember the sacrifice of your only son. Remember your covenant to us through His divine blood."

There are times during the Mass when we pray spontaneously. This is most evident around the time of receiving Jesus in the Eucharist. This is the moment of my life when I am truly closest to God and I pour my soul out to Him. Mass is the cornerstone of my prayer life. It is central to my life, the life of my family, and the life of my spiritual wellbeing. There is no prayer that is more important or that provides more grace. In Mass, my prayer transcends words and thoughts. In receiving the Eucharist (Christ's body, blood, soul, and divinity), my entire being, including my physical being, is in prayer to the Lord. He is *in* me, and I am *in* Him. It is similar to the deep communication, the deep communion, which occurs between a man and wife during the marital act. It is a complete and total giving of all aspects of self: mental, emotional, spiritual, and physical. There is no deeper communication than that.

Through prayer, the Lord has changed my life. He gives me ideas, answers questions, gives me tasks to accomplish, and reminds me of His love for me. I pray right now that the Lord remain with me during this current task. I pray that I write what He desires me to write. I ask for His blessing to rain down on all the readers of this book like a pure and beautiful snowfall, coating us in purity and renewal. I pray that we can all experience His peace and presence now and through all eternity. Amen.

to use the remaining time on this earth the Lord has given me to serve Him well.

It is an amazing thought that when I am in Mass, the church is full of legions of angels, praising and glorifying God with me. Members of our family that have made it to heaven pray with us throughout the sacrifice of the Mass and become one with us during our reception of Holy Communion.

Saints are not people who never sin. Saints are people who have fallen to sin but keep getting up! They never give up. They do not allow themselves to forfeit to despair. They do not "blaspheme the Holy Spirit" by denying in their lives the Mercy of God through the Cross! They do not allow themselves to become apathetic to sin. They have hope in God's mercy and thus hope in their salvation. **Ultimately, every saint has a past and every sinner has a future. YOU were created for sainthood!** It is that simple. Have you answered the call of that universal vocation? I often challenge myself, questioning if I am living a life worthy of that title.

I pray that I might learn from those who have gone before me. I pray that, through God's grace, I can one day join my brothers and sisters in the arms of our Lord. I look forward to meeting all the people that influenced my opportunity to see God. I am excited to meet my angels. I thank God for the saints!

Marriage

The first day I died to the "Religion of Self" in my life was the first day I decided that I love God and that I love my wife. I was in the ninth grade. Up to that point, every motivation I had in my life was for self. I studied hard in school so I could grow in wealth and power without working very hard. I played sports so I could attract women. I saved my money from hard work so I could buy myself a college education...so I could make more money. I played the piano and sang for attention. I cared purely and ultimately for self, self, self. I believed one day I would ultimately get married but that was not my problem at the time, so I did not care.

Growing up, God was not my first priority. My relationship with God was completely abstract. I felt because He was forgiving, I could really do anything and it did not really matter. Heaven was a guarantee because I did not kill anybody...right?

I started to understand that although God loves me, in order to *receive* the gift of His love, I needed a relationship with Him. It was then that *everything* about my motivations changed. As I started to *give my life to Him*, I started to open myself to the relationship vocation He had in store for me since the time of my creation. Through prayer, I found that I longed to share everything about myself to a woman in marriage. **I started to love this woman, and I did not even know her name.** I had no idea when I would even meet her. Regardless, every motivation I then had every day, was to prepare myself for that vocation; to prepare myself for her and my family to come.

I no longer served myself in every act of every day. In early high school, I started studying in school so I could provide for my family one day. I started playing sports so I could be at my physical best, as my body was not just my own, my body was my wife's and God's as well. I played piano and sang for His glory, so I could bring others to Him through song. The irony is that I was much better at everything when the motivation was not just about 'me.' I performed better on tests and did not mind work as much. I was much more at peace with the present.

It is with this mindset that I decided to save myself physically before marriage. Up to that point, many people tried to scare me out of extramarital sex (fornication). They would talk about pregnancy, STDs like AIDS, and other deterrents. The problem is that as they were talking to a teenager. I felt I was invincible. I felt consequences could only happen to somebody else. I also knew of people giving themselves away without obvious consequence so I thought I could get away with it as well. I have also never really operated in fear.

It was when I decided I loved my wife that waiting for marriage then made sense. As I just said, my body is God's and my wife's. Until I was married, how did I know who would be my wife? Even if I thought I loved someone, without the covenant, the commitment, the oath made and sealed through the wedding vows, how would I ever truly know that this was the spouse God created for me? Without those vows given to me by my wife, how would I truly trust her intentions? How many people have thought they met "the one" and it did not ultimately work out? The words "I promise to be good to you in good times and bad, in sickness and in health, I will love you and honor you all the days of my life" are powerful words. They are the heavenly seal on the relationship between man and woman. Those words form a *lasting* covenant.

The reality is that I have never, ever met two people, young or old, in marriage that are totally and completely in love with each other who would state to each other, "I am sooo glad you gave your body to someone else, the body meant for me since the beginning of time, to those other people before we were married. It just makes me feel so happy inside. Sleeping around was so great for our long-term commitment to each other..." **Extramarital sex is *always* an affront to a healthy, lasting marriage!** If you have fallen in this regard, there is hope...Repent. Accept the grace of the Cross. None of us are immune to sin.

In preparing for marriage, I knew that **my body was built *to celebrate* the sacrament of marriage**. Yes, you heard me right...You are not hallucinating! Just as being present at the liturgy of the Holy Mass renews our covenant with God, the *liturgy* of the marital act is an integral part of the renewal of our marriage covenant. Liturgy is an action that 1) Glorifies God 2) Sanctifies Man and 3) Builds the "Body of Christ." The marital act glorifies God as He is present and He gives us each other in marriage as a gift. The marital act itself *bestows sacramental grace* on the couple; In other words, it is healthy for a marriage and for one's spiritual well-being and therefore sanctifies man. And finally, as life can come from the act itself, it literally builds the "Body of Christ." – The marital act renews the Sacrament of Marriage – it is the physical manifestation of a spiritual reality.

> "This one, at last, is bone of my bones and flesh of my flesh. That is why a man leaves his father and mother and clings to his wife, and *the two of them become one body*." (Gen 2:23)

In marriage, I die to myself. The love I had in ninth grade for my wife, the same love I have today, is not some euphoric, lasting feeling. It is a daily, moment by moment *decision* to love my wife. It is a decision to die to myself for something greater. It is only through the death of myself that *relationship* with my spouse can even begin. That is why a groom wears all black during the wedding ceremony to symbolize death to himself.

Only then can I offer her everything that I am physically through the marital act. Through the same act, she is giving everything of herself to me. Again, we are celebrating a physical manifestation of a spiritual reality by renewing the Sacrament of Marriage. **That is why the marital act belongs in marriage!**

As going to Mass frequently is healthy to receive the sacramental grace of the Eucharist, **the frequent reception of sacramental grace through renewal of our marriage covenant is healthy** and can happen very often…Awesome!! Thank God!! Every married guy reading this chapter just said to himself, "This is the best book I have every read!!" I have a feeling this book will be pulled out and left on the night stand, opened to this page….

Now ladies, here is the part you have been waiting for. Death to self in marriage is not just experienced physically in the bedroom. Death to self is an attitude that works in *every* aspect of married life. The reality is that we are "making love" *all day*, by giving ourselves to each other in the sacrifice of changing diapers, going to work, folding the laundry, cutting the lawn, making meals, and yes – physically in the bedroom. It is one spoke on the wheel of a healthy marriage. Half the time in my human weakness, I feel like I would die for my spouse and my family, just don't ask me to get off the couch to empty the trash... Our kids understand that our relationship as husband and wife is the foundation of our relationships with them. They understand that a healthy marriage is one of the best gifts that we can give them. In that, they expect us to go away for 1 week a year as a couple alone and to have a date at least every 2 weeks.

Now some reading this will say to themselves, "I thought this guy was Catholic. He seems to be surprisingly casual about discussing his love life in marriage." The truth is that physical love in marriage is a great gift from God. **It is not some side-effect of creation that God 'tolerates' for the propagation of our species.** It is not like I praise God at every moment in my life and somehow try to hide from Him when I am celebrating my marriage with my wife. If anything, He is likely there at that moment more than most, as we are vulnerable through the giving of ourselves.

With some of the Catholic Faith, there is a distorted sexual philosophy where one should be ashamed of and embarrassed by marital love as was described well by Dr. Gregory Popcak when he described the disordered "Aunt Mcgillicuddy's Urn School of Sexuality."

"It grudgingly admits that sex is beautiful – in a grotesque, overdone, gothic sort of way – but above all, sex is holy and therefore, a little like Aunt Mcgillicuddy's antique urn; it must be approached delicately, cautiously, and (ideally) infrequently. That is, 'We oonly tooch it if we have to dust it, and then, oonly once a month or soo.'"

One day, during one of our infrequent trips to the mall with the entire family, with our children circling us like an entourage of humanity, we were approached by one of my wife's co-workers. She exclaimed, "Where did all of these children come from?!" I responded, "Saturday afternoon naps!" Her mouth dropped wide open. My oldest children busted out laughing. Mom and Dad's naps, talks, or whatever the code word for the day regarding the celebration of the marital act is part of our normal life at home.

Meanwhile, Satan has taken the great gift of marital love, and twisted it into an act of selfishness when it is not in the context of marriage. This distortion is what permeates most perceptions of sex. When holy people ascribe to Aunt Mcgillicuddy's guarded style, many people, especially teens, are never exposed to the holy *celebration and gift* that marital love represents. The truth is that marital love was the first commandment ordered by God Himself: "Be fertile and multiply; fill the earth and subdue it." (Gen 1:28) Yes folks, in the context of marriage, God is *commanding* us to go and have a good time with each other. Why should we be ashamed of or embarrassed by God's command and gift to us? Ultimately, we who clearly understand the *celebration* that marital love represents, need to stop tiptoeing around and stand out more publicly as a healthy *contrast* to Satan's distorted, selfish model of human sexuality.

As Elizabeth and I die to ourselves in marriage, *we are simultaneously opening our "one body" to the presence of God in our lives and our marriage.* Through God's sacramental grace of marriage, **we are the caretaker of each other's soul.** Our marriage becomes holy. **With the openness to the presence of God comes openness to life because God is Life**.

As God the Father eternally loves God the Son, God the Holy Spirit "proceeds" from that relationship. Therein lays the mystery of the Trinity. **Life is manifest in love as God is Life and God is Love. Creation and life is God just being God**.

Similarly, children given as gifts to parents are the walking, talking manifestation of the love the spouses have for each other. Repeatedly, throughout scripture, God's greatest gift to His faithful was the gift of children. Children are the fruit of love. Children are the reward of death to self and total self-giving in marriage. In our death to self, life is born. My wife and I have total abandonment to our lives, as we have given our life to God. This includes our fertility. Otherwise, I would be telling God and my wife, "Take my body and my life except I still want control of my fertility... I know more than you do about what is best for me."

Love builds on itself. It is not divided. It is not like I have a bucket of love that has to be split between my children. Rather, with my 8 children,

I am bursting with love for all of them! A vast majority of reasons to contracept are selfish. If you want a healthy relationship with God as a couple, communicate, pray and *be generous* – we need to die to ourselves. Ask yourself if contracepting is for God's Glory or not, and go from there.

Although all of the surfaces of my home are perpetually sticky with finger prints from last week's snack, with crayoned scribbling on the walls, and despite the reality that kids entail a lot of suffering, they bring with them genuine relationship, life, goodness, community, and ultimately a glimpse of Heaven with God in the Trinity, personalities and all. They bring Trust and Love. My children are all very different, and therefore bring out different parts of me as a man. Most the time, I am learning about myself, while trying to parent them through the challenges of life. It is good to be a father!

All the principles discussed in this chapter also apply to vocations of those who are single and those called to the religious life. Single life is most definitely not an "inferior" vocation to marriage. In fact, it is quite the opposite. St. Paul stated it accurately, "It is better to be single, only proceed with marriage if you must." (1Cor7:27) I did not understand that statement until I got married. Before I was married, the Lord would say "jump" and I would ask "how high?" Since marriage, the Lord says "jump" and I turn to my wife and ask "Honey, how high are *we* going to jump?"

Those called to the vocation of single consecrated life or religious life need to also die to themselves and give themselves totally and completely to their 'spouse,' who is God. For a priest, he serves his spouse by serving his parish. For a single person, they serve their spouse by serving the community at large.

Lord, I pray that we can find the vocation you have set forth for us in our life. I pray that we can die to ourselves so we can be open to your will. In our vocation, help us further to die to ourselves so we can serve each other. I pray to be a good husband and father. Mold me into the man you expect me to be. I am yours.

Results of the Religion of Self

This chapter may be hard to read for some. **The Truth should be able to withstand opposition.... Otherwise it is not True. Those who seek the Truth find *rest* in it, not anxiety.**

One day, before going to a wise priest in confession, I spent 3 weeks making a speech about a grey area in my life that I was hoping to justify so I could continue the behavior. During confession, the priest sat and listened intently as I delivered one of the best speeches of my entire life. It was well thought out and perfectly articulate, if I might say so myself!... After I finished, there was at least 5 seconds of silence. He then sat up in the front of his chair, looked me dead in the eye and yelled out as loudly as he could, "BULLLLLLLLLLLLLLLSHIIIIIIIIIIIT!!!!!!" I laughed pretty hard. I love that guy.... I need someone to call me out on the BS in my life, to push me to be better than I would be on my own. Iron sharpens iron.

In talking to an older gentleman who was married for over 50 years, I asked him, "What was the trick?" He stated, "We just stayed married.".... (Another man just stated after 75 years of marriage that "Weeee juuust liiived for a verrrrrrrry looong tiiiime.)

That is the Truth. Our lives change in time. We are faced with many challenges that we cannot foresee. Our feelings for our spouse wax and wane throughout time. We love them, but are not always attracted to them. We are faced with personality differences that are sometimes not ever resolved. Sometimes we encounter others that are more compatible in personality than our spouse and we are tempted. The *feeling* of love is not always there... But actual love is not a feeling at all. It is a day by day, moment by moment choice...In good times *and* bad, in sickness and

112

health.... As a couple grows together in time, and the choice to love each other is made, the union deepens and deepens, along with the peace and joy and grace that accompanies that union.

Marriage is a covenant. Covenants are a lasting promise. If my wife chose to leave me in divorce, it would pull apart the very fabric of my being and I would die as the man that I am because I am her and she is me. The vows establishing a covenant in marriage is why divorce is not allowed in the Catholic Church and condemned by God.

"Some Pharisees approached him, and tested him saying, 'Is it lawful for a man to divorce his wife for *any* cause whatever?' He (Jesus) said in reply, 'Have you not read that from the beginning the Creator 'made them male and female' and said, 'For this reason a man shall leave his father and mother and be joined to his wife, and the two shall become one flesh?' So they are no longer two, but one flesh. Therefore, what God has joined together, no human must separate." (Mt 19:3)

Jesus spoke against divorce in all four Gospels. He was not vague about this topic at all. That said, a couple maintains individual free-will in marriage and sadly, can choose not to love the other, or to ultimately die to themself. Therefore, although a Catholic marriage remains valid, the couple does not need to live together and can become separated, especially if abuse is present. The Catholic Church would strongly encourage a couple to attempt reconciliation, even in cases of infidelity. Ultimately a civil (legal) divorce for the separation of property may be needed, yet spiritually, a married couple is still married, whether they live together or not because marriage is a covenant.

> "Whoever divorces his wife (unless the marriage is unlawful) causes her to commit adultery, and whoever marries a divorced woman commits adultery. Again you have heard that it was said to your ancestors, 'Do not take a false oath, but make good to the Lord all that you vow.'" (Mt 5:32)

Choosing a divorce is selfish. Yes, Christ's teaching on divorce is a tough teaching because it takes 2 people to choose to be married. One can do everything they possibly can to remain married, but nobody has power over another's will. Although the Church's teaching is tough, it is true. It is tough, as the call to perfection and Sainthood is also tough. The Church sets the bar of perfection for us. It must not allow that bar to be dropped to our weaknesses, otherwise, what would we have to strive to? The lowest expectation? I am glad there is a bar of perfection for us to strive for, even though I often do not reach it myself.

Again, in the "Religion of Self," marriage is typically avoided at all costs because successful marriage promotes death to self. In the "Religion of Self" children are an absolute threat and burden. In the "Religion of Self," relationship and the community of the family is *anathema*. Hence, in a world of "self," extra-marital sex has become the norm. This non-committed lifestyle is selfish. Abortion is perceived to be needed. And in the world of "self," the very concept of marriage is under attack.

Because the "Religion of Self" is so deeply rooted in our culture, when people are getting married after years of extramarital relationships and co-habitation where they pretend they are married, it frequently ends in divorce. Why? Because the "Religion of Self" is brought into the marriage. These couples are accustomed to leaving *pretend* marriages repeatedly before actually marrying. Why would that habit of leaving when challenges arise magically disappear when one finally ties the knot in marriage, especially if they are still living for themself? In marrying a spouse who had a similar pre-marriage experience, real trust would be hard to establish because there would always seem to be one foot out the door. It is like playing a game of "chicken" with their spouse because one would always maintain an emotional wall, not offering too much of themself in the fear that the pain would be that much worse if the relationship ended as so many prior relationships had ended.

As marriages are ending at an alarming rate, the children of these unions are often left without a stable, parental upbringing by both a mother *and* a father. Kids are simple. They do not need money. They need safety and love. In some situations where the child's safety is threatened or there is no love present, being raised by a single parent may be necessary, but it is most definitely NOT the ideal. "It takes a village to raise a child" is total nonsense. Since the first existence of man, it takes only a mother *and* father.

In reading "Sex Matters" (Mona Charen 2018) Study after study relates that as a global overview, being raised by both a man and a woman is the *single largest predictor* of whether one will live in poverty, go further in education, will avoid prison, will be raised in a "safe and stable home," and will ultimately raise their own children as a couple.

Racism is often mistakenly blamed when race is viewed in these statistics. This makes no sense whatsoever when one correlates single parenting into the discussion. Minorities that have the highest single parent ratio have the highest poverty rate, crime rate, incarcerations and so forth. Whites are in the middle statistically regarding this issue. Minorities with the lowest single parent ratio are the most likely to succeed, including comparing themselves to their white peers and other minorities.

In running Camp Veritas, a camp for thousands of teens each year, 75% of my *difficult* kids have an absent father figure (The other 25 percent just behave like idiots for no apparent reason). The boys have no paternal role models to emulate and are forced to make it up as they go along. They love their mothers but do not "fear" them in respect. The girls in this group are starving for male attention. They often fill the hole left by their absent father with perpetual boyfriends and the drama that accompanies this lifestyle. Most have a low self-esteem.

I have 6 sisters, 5 daughters, a 100% staff of women, and 75% of the patients I see each day are women. I have seen over 100,000 patients. I have noticed a theme. Most women are asking, "Where have all of the men gone?"

The following is pure personal observation, not a national study. As the family unit is crumbling under the "Religion of Self," and we have a generation raised by "the village," the normal family unit led by mom and dad is therefore questioned as even necessary. This theory of attempting to normalize single parenting began with the feminist movement of the 1960's, where in order to free woman from the "shackles" of marriage, men were errantly deemed to be unnecessary. This was also the time of the sexual revolution and the normalization of atheism. There are 4 effects of this that I have seen.

Ryan Young

1) Without belief in an all present God, with the Religion of Self increasing as fast as Atheism, men no longer have accountability for their character "in the dark," when nobody is watching.

2) With the absence of fathers at home or the example of masculinity anywhere, for two generations, men are struggling to find good paternal role models and heroes.

3) Women are not holding men accountable prior to marriage to be better than they would be on their own, the reward of which is marriage and physical availability. Formerly, a man would have to prove that he would sacrifice himself for his bride, be a good father, provide for the family, and be a good leader before he experienced the reward of physical union with the woman with whom he was interested. Now he only has to buy dinner or "swipe right." This causes men to be perpetually immature. In the world of feminine competition, this also forces women to be more physically available.

4) Some women who believe they are "strong" think that strength must mean that they are never, ever, ever, to disorder, ever wrong and treat all men within 20 yards of themselves as inferior. They are great women in the world of family logistics, worldly success and productivity and they would claim that they fiercely love their husbands and children; however, they do not support their husbands in their masculinity as leaders or respect their decisions – it is a control thing. Most of these women can never apologize and marry weak men who are beaten into the "Yes Dear" mentality, but cease to be strong men. The men then either exist as another older child or servant boy of this "strong" woman, or leave her 20 years into marriage with any woman who treats them as men. I work with plenty of female clients who are in this category.

Men, we need to find our voices with some confidence and become _the leaders_ we were built to be. This is both at home and the community at large. None of the 75,000 women I have encountered over the past 20 years are _attracted to_ weak "Yes Dear" men. They will marry them only because there are no real men left. The women will lead the family unit, although most would state that at home, they would rather not have this burden.

This authority is not license to become a tyrant. We need to love women and serve them as princesses of God. We need to lay down our lives every day for our families. We need to communicate well and respect

116

those we serve. We need to love. We need to lead our families to God. That is our greatest responsibility.

Women, if you want men to return to their *natural design* of self-sacrifice, start encouraging them to be men. Tell them flat out that you will not respect them unless they have the capacity to lead and make decisions. Give up some control. Appreciate and encourage masculinity and its role in our society and culture. Voice the need for men in family life and the community. Don't settle for weak men. Encourage other women to do the same.

The transgender movement is another result of the Religion of Self. Remember the discussion in the beginning about either accepting a Truth bigger than self – There is a God and I am not Him – or leaving Reality and making up the illusion we see fit. There is no more obvious symptom of this than the transgender movement. Not only does one leave reality in the movement, but worse, many will label all who do not join them in their delusion as "Haters" "Bigots" "Intolerant" "Transphobes" or whatever label there is to bully and control. What is *the principle* of the movement? That we can all leave reality and just be whatever we please? Why not be a chimpanzee or a poodle? We all have great imaginations. Right now, in the state of NY, if you don't accept other's delusions, you can be charged with "Sexual Harassment" and fired from your job.

The biggest lie in the whole subject, created by Satan himself, is the lie that unless you accept every thought of every person around you as equal, that *you do not love them.*

One day as a speaker, I mentioned the above at a men's conference. There was strong and somewhat loud affirmation until I said the second half of the statement….: "Those Catholics who are buffet Catholics and believe only some of what the Catholic Church teaches, but refuse to believe the entire Truth of the Church's teachings, are doing the same thing as those in the transgender movement. They are making up an illusion where they can be their own god, personalizing reality, answering to no other authority other than self." Well, the room got pretty quiet after that.

The celebration of illusion is only affirmed by our society at large. Our entire culture is leaving Reality en masse. Our culture realizes that if they do not support every delusion, their own made up world might be questioned through the "Religion of Self." I love those with gender confusion as much as I love all of those in their illusion (which is most people until they find God).

The transgender movement is NOT the same as the challenge of same sex attraction. Those with same-sex attraction may be living in the actual *reality* of that attraction. Many of those with same-sex attraction "tolerate" the extra BTQ's (LGBTQ.....)for political purposes.

If you haven't noticed, I am a fairly blunt guy. I also truly love those who suffer from same sex attraction. I have many patients and co-workers with this struggle. It is a real cross. Those with authentic same sex attraction get along with me just fine, usually because they know and appreciate very early on that I too, am authentic, even if we don't agree on everything. More than anything, they also know without a doubt that I love them! I would die for them! And frankly, I would suspect that they would be the first to die for me if the occasion arose. In general, those with genuine same sex attraction realize that it is rare and they are not insecure. In conversations that I have had with those with this authentic struggle, they realize their disorder is a disorder but have accepted it, throwing themselves at the Mercy of God if they choose to *act* on it. We all have our struggles. Get in line....

What is ironic is that while some people have authentic same sex attraction and choose to pick up their cross with Christ and lead a saintly life of self-control and self-mastery, with avoidance of acting out on their attractions, others have made same sex attraction a FAD, a completely commercialized attention-seeking FAD, and totally *inauthentic*. As the "father of thousands" each summer at Camp Veritas, I have observed a growing trend with the youth. I grew up in the 80's. At that time, in order to get attention, teens would color their hair purple, get a tattoo, get into trouble, and so forth. Now, we all know the teen who one random day "comes out of the closet" wearing a rainbow flag, carrying a rainbow bright backpack, with rainbow socks, suddenly becoming flamboyantly effeminate, prancing around the school throwing confetti, having their social media explode in rainbow fireworks, while screaming to the universe with every action, thought, and post, "I am soooooooooo gaaaaaaaay!!!!" The first thing they say to everybody within 3 sentences of their presence,

"Hi, I'm gay... Did you know I am gay?.... Did you know?!.... Look at me.... Look at me.... Look at me...."

Our societal response to this attention-seeking FAD is a *standing ovation* with congratulations and gross encouragement. If we stopped the standing ovation, I suspect the amount of people with same sex attraction would again drop to the normal, rare level. The Truth is that I pity those who feel like this FAD is the only way to be noticed. They are searching and really screaming quietly, "Look at me... Before this charade, nobody even knew I was around. I must not be worthy of love." Those with authentic same-sex attraction normally don't need to talk about it to everybody because they realize their attraction is NOT their identity. We all have challenges.

Meanwhile, I can name numerous individuals that I grew up with who were brutal and hateful in their obsession about those with same sex attraction in the locker room setting who finally admitted after years of public hate that they themselves had the same attraction! They were in an internal battle, hating themselves while the rest of us got to witness this struggle.

Having same-sex attraction is **not** a sin in and of itself. Yet, we should not encourage our brothers and sisters to *act* in sin either. Same sex attraction *is a disorder*. If it wasn't and was the order of creation, we would not exist. Let me tell you a secret...We are all disordered!! Some people have a tendency to lie. Others have an inclination to gossip. Others struggle with the disorders of gluttony, anorexia, fornication, or alcoholism. Others have more serious disorders like pedophilia. Same sex attraction is, therefore, not a *license to sin,* to act upon those disordered instincts.

> "Let the one among you who is without sin be the first to throw a stone at her"... "Woman, where are they? Has no one condemned you?... Neither do I condemn you. Go, *and from now on do not sin anymore.*"(Jn8:7)

The Catholic Church has always promoted self-control, self-physical mastery. This includes self-control in marriage. This includes self-control for the clergy and for those who are single. Why is there a call for an exemption with those who have same sex attraction? We are not animals.

Human beings can make conscious decisions that defy animal instincts. That consciousness is what sets humans apart from animals. Again, this is a hard reality for some. We all fall, but we <u>must get up</u> again and again. Those with same sex attraction are called to single life. They are called to love others *as we are all called* to love others. Like all others, they are called to physical self-control within their vocation in life. That self-control is also necessary in marriage to avoid pornography, adultery, and abstinence at times to space births if necessary. No matter what, no matter where we are in the struggle, it should be toward God, holding His hand in the struggle of chastity and self-control.

The next symptom of the Religion of Self is suicide. It is the fastest growing cause of death in the country, of all ages. There are many reasons for this. Almost everybody has been affected by this growing trend. In dealing with suicidal teens for years at camp, I have found several common themes here as well.

1) Some contemplate suicide because they are in pain in a desert and cannot see an end to their pain so they make their own way out. Part of being in the desert is not knowing when it will end, otherwise, it would not be a desert. Despair is not of God. Hope is. **God does not live in the past in guilt. He does not live in the future in anxiety. He lives in the present..... Right now.. Every desert ends eventually. God's grace will get you through anything.**

2) Others commit suicide as an act of revenge against those they love. Revenge is never from God.

3) Others have this romantic idea of "Being with Jesus now because they love Him." You don't want to see Jesus when he is disappointed and angry with you because you did not receive the gift He had for you in life.

To those who are contemplating suicide right now while reading this book – Suicide is the ultimate act of Pride. It is telling God, "I know more than you do about how long this precious life should last." Committing suicide is like walking out of a difficult test in school without finishing the end of the test. The grade is never very good in that circumstance. Suicide robs the world of your unique greatness, your saintly potential. Suicide damages *generations* of your family. *It will never actually be looked at as a natural death. It will be hard for most to celebrate a life that was intentionally thrown away.* Suicide is selfish! If you are contemplating suicide, by definition you are under extreme spiritual and psychological attack. GET HELP NOW!! Find a trusted friend, counselor, mentor, priest, nun, mom, dad. Anyone who can listen and take you seriously.

To those who have lost somebody to suicide. Like everyone we lose, trust in the Mercy of God. Pray for the deceased. It is most definitely OK and normal to be angry about it, but don't let that anger consume you. Give the pain to God. Let it go. The Father grieved the loss of His Son on the Cross.

There are many other symptoms of the Religion of Self in our time. I picked the headlining ones in order to arm those on the front line of Reality with a shield of reason and a sword of Truth. Apply the principles addressed here and don't forget that *we need to love all first.* Only then will any consideration and change be possible.

Life

She graduated from college and is going to law school. She looks like an angel from heaven. In her early childhood she had blond ringlets that would have made Shirley Temple jealous. She has almond brown eyes that are the doorway to her soul. She enjoys boys and her circle of girlfriends. She gets straight A's in school (quietly) and is mature beyond her years. She loves to paint and draw. She enjoys softball and surfing. She loves her dog and her parents. She would say she has had a great life. She has dreams of her future and has ambition and goals. She is loved by all who encounter her. She is the kind of young lady that would seek out and befriend the new kid in class, not because she lacked friends, but because it is her nature. She is the joy of so many that have had the privilege to know her. Some day she will make a man very happy in marriage. They will have children of their own and grandchildren and great-grandchildren. It is through this life of hers that generations of lives will inherit such goodness, such peace and love. This great life, this fantastic person was a hairs-breadth from an early death.

Life simply cannot be imagined if she were not here. All who have encountered this young lady would not have experienced how bright and wonderful this life on Earth can be if she was not a part of it.

Meanwhile, the mother-to-be of this young lady grew up in a culture which bombarded her with values contrary to Catholic teaching. As her own value system formed, she came to believe that sexual intimacy was to be reserved until you found someone "you love." However, there was never an expectation of holding onto that gift until reaching the commitment of marriage. As a result, at age sixteen, this teenager gave herself for the first time to her boyfriend of several years. She happened to be fertile and thus became pregnant.

When she first became aware of her situation, she told her boyfriend and his parents. They immediately went into a state of denial. They simply refused to accept that reality. They just hoped the situation would disappear. They wouldn't allow their son to speak to her or associate with her in any way. The boyfriend's parents and her boyfriend simply abandoned her in her time of need.

Meanwhile, something had to be done. There was the obvious problem: this 16-year-old, pregnant teenager was afraid to tell her parents. She was fearful that they would never understand. What if they rejected her also? What if they kicked her out of the house? She felt completely alone.

Desperate thoughts filled her mind. She knew there was a way out. All she had to do was have an abortion. No one would know. It would solve all of her problems. She could continue life like nothing had happened.

Then God intervened. Grace abounded. Truth kissed her. Suddenly she was enlightened and saw the problem clearly. If she had an abortion, *she* would know; *God* would know. She could never escape herself. She would never be able to look herself in the eye again. Her maternal instinct screamed to her that if she were to destroy the child inside her, she would be destroying a part of her own soul.

She waited until her father was not around before she told her mother. Her mother was supportive. Together they decided to tell her father when he was away on business and thousands of miles away from home. Distance would be a protective buffer.

They called her father. Much to their surprise, there was no explosion. There were no threats. The father immediately began to help. Inspired by the Spirit, he contacted his married brother. His brother and his brother's wife had wanted children for years but could not have them naturally. This was an answer to their prayers!

The pregnant teenager was invited to live with her aunt and uncle during the ensuing months. Finally the teenage mother gave birth to her beautiful, baby girl who was then immediately adopted by the mother's aunt and uncle. It is through this "bad" situation that tremendous goodness was released into the world. Although the child was initially unintended by this couple, this child was *not* unintended by God. This young teenage girl gave her aunt and uncle the love of their lives. The child has, and hopefully will continue to have, a great life. The teenage mother faced adversity and, with God's grace, triumphed. In delivering that child, the teenage mother for the first time in her life realized that God is *real*! In carrying her cross, she *experienced* God's love for her. She died to herself and became resurrected into a woman of honor, character, dignity, and strength. In her fall, with her determination to get back up, she understood her call to be a saint. She was being molded by God for her true love in her marriage to come. She was being prepared for her soul-mate. She was being prepared to become *my wife*. There are no accidents.

The fateful day my wife chose to allow her child to live, over 1,700 women in the United States faced that same decision and made a tragic mistake. Undoubtedly most of these women are good people, perhaps even holy people. But in their moment of distress, in their moment of abandonment, they are "helped" by parents, doctors, and friends who have bought into the biggest lie of our age. These misguided helpers with their *misdirected compassion*, these unwitting accomplices to the "Father of Lies", convince these young pregnant women to abort their own babies. After all, they argue, it is the "right" of the mother to terminate her pregnancy. The unborn baby has no rights. The unborn baby has not yet achieved 'personhood'; the unborn baby is really only a fetus. It is only a very small, unimportant glob of tissue.

The following chapter is an areligious discussion of reason and logic. It is to prepare you for the discussion that inevitably occurs at the dinner table, at most institutions of education, and with those of all faiths and backgrounds. We must all seek the Truth in this issue. Too much is at stake to put our heads in the sand and pretend that there is not a problem.

Society must acknowledge that the unborn are genetically human. Human women do not deliver dogs or elephants or carrots or fish. Society must also agree that the unborn entity is "alive." Unborn people, like born people, are composed of cells that are growing, reproducing, metabolizing, developing and living.

Our society and justice system made a law in Roe vs. Wade that doesn't allow that unborn, human, alive, child to achieve '*personhood*' until the unborn child has fully passed through some invisible magical force-field in the birth canal. Without personhood, even though the unborn child is alive and human, the unborn child is not protected under our laws.

It is therefore fully legal to experiment on the child or use that child's nervous system as spare parts for the handicapped in "embryonic stem cell research." It is also fully legal to burn the skin off of this unborn child with chemicals until they bleed to death, dismember this child by sharp surgical instruments, and eviscerate this child through high powered suction and blending. It is even legal during delivery to stab a partially born alive and moving child in the back of the skull and remove the child's brains while the child is still in the birth canal and collapse her skull. This "partial birth abortion" is legal as long as a portion of the child's body remains in the mother. Five seconds later, when the child is completely outside the birth canal, stabbing the child is considered murder. *Have we completely lost our minds?*

Legal abortion is not the first time that genocide was justified by denying the personhood of alive, human beings. Hitler justified the Holocaust because the Jews were not classified as 'persons' under German law. Our United States Supreme Court justified slavery through the "Dred Scott Decision" whereby African-Americans were not given 'personhood' and were therefore enslaved like livestock. There has never been a time in human history when mankind has been correct when separating the status of 'personhood' from alive, human beings.

That is why the Catholic Church, long before our Declaration of Independence, identified all human beings as having the inalienable rights of "life, liberty, and the pursuit of happiness." Inalienable rights are rights that we don't have to earn. They are rights that are inherent to us because we *exist* and because of our respect for human life and human dignity. The most basic of these rights is the *right to life* because, without it, all other rights are irrelevant. If you are dead, your other rights are of little value.

Ironically, the 'personhood' of the child in modern culture is based solely on whether or not the mother *wants* the child to be a person. The unborn child is protected under the laws *if* the mother wants to 'keep her baby.' For example, if a pregnant woman is murdered, the murderer gets charged with two counts of murder. What is unbelievable about this is that the mother can, at any time, go and kill that child in an abortion and our society will subsidize that abortion through Planned Parenthood. Does this make any sense to anybody?

If a mother looks at her child and decides that she does not want her child to be a person anymore, does that child objectively cease to be a child? If that same woman looked at a tree and declared that it was not a tree, does the tree objectively cease to be a tree? Why do different principles apply to the unborn?

At what stage of development does the unborn child become a person? The pro-abortionist would argue that at any time during the nine months before birth the unborn child "has not yet developed into a human-being." They would claim that in the first few weeks and months of life the unborn child is "just a few cells."

My retort is that a child is *supposed* to be a few cells at that age. My 10-year-old does not look the same as he had when he was a 5-year-old or when he was a 2-year-old. We are all still developing and will be until death. This development started at conception. Genetically, everything you are right now was present at that first cell. *Life did not begin after the child passed through the magical, invisible force field in the birth canal.* A one-day-old, unborn, one-celled child is supposed to go through that normal stage of human development. This logic is also true of a more developed three-week-old unborn child and an even more developed eight-month-old. That is normal human development. Everyone reading this chapter was once a one-celled unborn child that continued growing *before* and *after* birth. In short, the act of birth did not cause development to cease. Therefore, the argument that the child isn't "developed" is not applicable.

If 'personhood' is to be assigned at some random moment of development, what happened in that moment of time that justifies that conclusion? For example, if 'the line' is at 3 months for the unborn, is the child truly not the same at 2 months, 29 days, 23hrs and 59 minutes? Of course the child is the same! The moment is arbitrary. If you were to ask, "What is the difference in a child as we go back in time, second by second?" the answer is the same. Nothing! You would find yourself having to start at conception to assign the title of personhood.

Some argue, "How do we have the right to tell a woman what she can or cannot do with *her* body?" We would then have to logically conclude that a woman carrying an unborn baby boy therefore has a penis, not to mention 2 brains, 2 hearts, 4 eyes, and 20 fingers and toes.

Some argue for abortion by saying that the child might be "born into a poor environment." If abortion is compassionate for the poor, why discriminate? The same principle should be applied to all the poor and we should then be 'compassionately' eliminating everybody we consider to be poor.

Some argue that the child might be handicapped. If that is the principle, we should consider 'compassionately' killing all those who have handicaps now. How ridiculous is it for us to judge whose life should start or end? My niece who has Downs Syndrome is one of the sweetest kids I know. Working with those in the Special Olympics, I found that these individuals with handicaps were the most joy-filled people I have ever met in my life. At times, I envy their innocence and purity.

In short, for whatever 'compassionate' reason abortion is justified, the same principle should then apply to those of us fortunate enough to have passed through the magical, invisible force-field of the birth canal.

Every time my wife is pregnant, we hear the comment from good hearted people: "as long as the baby is healthy…" I have always thought to myself, "and if they are not?" There are no guarantees in life. My children might get into a car accident or become ill at any time. Would I be expected to abort them then?

Some people are confused because abortion has been made legal. They have unwittingly fallen into the moral trap that "since an act is legal, it is therefore moral." I recently viewed on Amazon Prime television a documentary of the one child policy in China which was instituted in 1979. (One Child Nation 2019) In the documentary, it described in detail that families who had a second child would simply go to the market and leave their child there while thousands of people would go about their daily business shopping at the market. These infants would sit there for days, crying and ignored until they would die from exposure. Some infants were simply left on the side of the road like roadkill, but were still alive as thousands of people would simply walk by leaving them to die. Other babies were taken alive from their mother's body by the "population control officer" of their town through forced abortion and the child was either strangled to death, or their throats would be slashed.

When asked, "How could you leave your own child in the market like that?" They would respond, "The policy is the policy. What else could we do?" When children are legally aborted at term here in NY, truly, *are we any different?!!*

Many focus on the 3% of abortions done for medical reasons or rape and incest and therefore turn a blind eye to the other 97% of abortions done strictly with the mindset of birth control.

In regards to rape and incest, abortions done for these reasons are about 1%. Studies have proven that when a woman has an abortion after a rape, she still suffers from post-abortion syndrome. In many ways, having that abortion is like allowing that rapist to control her again. The child also didn't ask to be there. If the child of the rapist was born and standing in front of us, could we justify killing the child then? There are many families that would be more than willing to adopt that child and, in a way, the mother of that child could live the rest of her life knowing the rapist didn't turn *her* into a murderer. In the end she defeated evil and turned a negative situation into a positive one.

Consider the mother that has an abortion for medical reasons. The Catholic Church is clear in this situation. If the mother's *life* is in jeopardy during a pregnancy, *her* life is not less valuable than the life of her child. The effort should then to be to save *both* the mother and child, even if that means delivering the child early and doing our best to save that child. This approach holds even if the odds of rescue are slim. We should still give the child a chance at pulling through. If there was an avalanche that buried skiers, we would still search for them even if the odds of survival are low and the path treacherous. If the mother had cancer and needed chemotherapy which would be harmful to the unborn child, it would still be permissible as her intention would be to treat the cancer, not to harm her child.

The same reasoning applies to the treatment of an ectopic pregnancy. An ectopic pregnancy is the situation whereby an unborn child implants somewhere other than uterus, often in the fallopian tube. If that portion of the fallopian tube is not removed, *both* mother and child would die. Removal of that abnormal portion of the fallopian tube is essential to prevent the same situation from occurring again. The *intention* is never to kill the child although that is the inevitable outcome. The mom's life is not worth less than her child's. The intention should be to save the lives of both, in all circumstances, if possible.

Pay attention to our politicians as they discuss this however. The pro-abortionists don't discuss the '*life*' of the mother; they discuss the '*health*' of the mother. Health has been defined by the Supreme Court in Doe vs. Bolton as "mental, psychological, emotional, or financial health." **Abortion is legal until *birth* in all states of this country if the mother's 'health' is in question**. In other words, at nine months gestation, at which time the mother could have a c-section, she can legally abort her child if she states that she is depressed or not financially 'healthy.' In NY, one does not even have to pass the test of 'health.' They can simply have abortion on demand at any point till birth simply because the woman wants to and she has the right as a woman to kill her child, no questions asked.

In embryonic stem cell research, our country has compassion for those who are ill or handicapped. Through that 'misdirected compassion,' we are legalizing experimentation on the unborn and the use of their parts. What I would like answered by Michael J. Fox and his followers is the question: "How many children are you willing to slaughter for their parts so you don't have Parkinson's disease anymore? 1,000? 100? 10? 1?" Again, are we going to allow the ends to justify the means?

Some argue that this is a private issue and the government should stay out of it. If that same child was born and lived in the privacy of the woman's home, and the woman was burning off her child's skin or stabbing the back of the child's skull with a scissors, wouldn't the child's right to life supersede that woman's right to privacy?

What does this mean? The truth of this matter is hard to comprehend. Although the numbers of children aborted has been decreasing for a decade, nearly as many children are killed *every single day* in this country than those who were killed on the 9/11/2001 Twin Tower attack in New York City. More children are killed in our country *every other year* than have died in all wars America has ever fought. More than 50,000,000 lives have been slaughtered in this contemporary American Holocaust. Why?

It all comes down to the most predominant "religion" in the United States today: *The Religion of Self.* Abortion is just a symptom of the mindset of our time. We want to live a life without consequence. This includes, of course, our sexual life. We want to have 'the freedom' to have sex with anything that breathes and not have to worry about consequences. Again, children are a perceived threat for the quest of power and control. Children are perceived by many as a burden. Our society therefore continues to ignore the blatant Truth and the magnitude of the abortion problem.

We literally have no orphanages in the USA because there is no such thing as an unwanted child here. As the age of wanting children is becoming later and later, there is a dramatic increase in infertility in our 30's. People are flying all over the world and paying tens of thousands of dollars to adopt children, meanwhile the abortion clinic is killing thousands of kids daily because people are too selfish to go through a pregnancy.

Instead of cherishing our woman and honoring them in their femininity and supporting them when they are pregnant, with abortion we destroy that which distinguishes woman from men. The feminist movement is actually pushing that a woman is somehow "less than a woman" if she is unwilling to slaughter her own children. We attack every fiber of maternal instinct and minimize the human life growing inside of her as "just a blob of cells." In essence, we are all just a blob of cells. Abortion and embryonic stem cell research are evil. **Abortion and embryonic stem cell research are acts that are *always* rooted in selfishness. They are wrong, every time, always... period.**

The Catholic Church defines abortion as "gravely immoral."(CCC 2272) In participating in an abortion, whether having one, advising friends or family to have an abortion, promoting the abortion cause, or intentionally voting for politicians who advance abortion in our society, one is placing on oneself a "lampshade of sin" thick enough to block out the light, that is, the life of grace given to us. We become separated from God.

As was mentioned, 1,700 kids are aborted daily in the USA alone. *Think* of how many people you know who may have had an abortion. Think of how many boyfriends and fathers and parents and friends were instrumental in encouraging that act. Perhaps one of the reasons why abortion still exists in this country is that there is a subconscious, mistaken belief that since "everyone is doing it", and we live in a democracy, we are safe from personal responsibility and the judgment of God. To correct the error it would take countless people to practice humility and have the capacity to admit making a massive mistake. Most find it simply easier to pretend nothing is wrong. It would seem that many are afraid of having participated in this level of evil, and therefore feel the urge to fight to keep the lie alive. It would be like being a German who sought out Jews to send to a concentration camp or working in the concentration camp itself and deciding later that they participated in a holocaust of human life.

For those who have participated in abortion, welcome to sinful humanity. We have all fallen. Abortion is not the only sin out there. We all need the Cross. God is merciful. The light of God in all of our lives is always on, waiting for us to repent and remove the "lampshades" we have placed over His light. In repentance and humility, we have the ability to allow the grace of the Cross of Christ back in our lives and we can once again be set free of this great burden of sin. Jane Roe (from Roe v. Wade), whose real name is Norma McCorvey, understood this and repented. She became aware of how she was "used" by those with misdirected compassion to further their cause. That is why she became a Christian and is now a leader in the fight to end abortion. She is a hero and is now seeking holiness. She is on the path that can lead to eternity with God. Finding this path and staying on it is the goal of every saint. Every saint has entered this path at a different point in his or her life, usually found through humility and repentance.

What now? I had to first accept the gravity of the present situation, especially politically. Does it really matter if I have a perfect candidate in every other issue such as gun control, taxes, education, health care, and national defense if that candidate is for the slaughter of 1,700 children *each* day? Does the importance of any other issue come remotely close? Readers, please consider making the end of abortion a top priority by voting for the candidate that is most pro-life, whether that candidate is a Republican or a Democrat, or an Independent

Secondly, use your voice. Speak for the unborn as they cannot speak for themselves. Talk to anyone who will listen. Encourage uniting those looking to abort their children with the thousands upon thousands of couples flying all over the world to adopt a child because there are so few children left here at home to adopt.

Thirdly, pray. After that, pray some more. Pray for a conversion of hearts. Pray for an end to the Religion of Self. Pray for awareness to the Truth. Pray for God to have mercy. Become a light in this time of darkness.

The good news is that, like the end of slavery and the end of the Jewish Holocaust, mankind ultimately comes to its senses. The question is: how many tens of millions of children will be slaughtered in the interim? How many souls of the living will die spiritually as a result of this atrocity? And the final question we should ask ourselves: *will I be able to look at my grandchildren in the eyes and state that I did everything in my power to stop this bloodshed?*

Stewardship

To summarize Christ's parable in Mt 25:14-30

"For the kingdom of heaven is like a man traveling to a far country, who called his own servants and delivered his goods to them. And to one he gave five talents, to another two, and to another one talent, to each according to his own ability; Then he who had received the five talents went and traded with them, and made another five talents. And likewise, he who had received two gained two more also. But he who had received one went and dug in the ground, and hid his lord's money. After a long time the lord of those servants came and settled accounts with them.

"So, he who had received five talents came and brought five other talents, saying, 'Lord, you delivered to me five talents; look, I have gained five more talents besides them.' He also who had received two talents came and said, 'Lord, you delivered to me two talents; look, I have gained two more talents besides them.' His lord said to them, 'Well done, good and faithful servants; you have been faithful over a few things, I will make you ruler over many things. Enter into the joy of your lord.'

"Then he who had received the one talent came and said, 'I was afraid, and went and hid your talent in the ground. Look, there you have what is yours.'"

"But his lord answered and said to him, 'You wicked and lazy servant, you ought to have deposited my money with the bankers, and at my coming I would have received

133

back my own with interest. Therefore, take the talent from him, and give it to him who has ten talents.

'For to everyone who has, more will be given, and he will have abundance; but from him who does not have, even what he has will be taken away. And cast the unprofitable servant into the outer darkness. There will be weeping and gnashing of teeth.'"

Growing up as one of nine children, my parents could not afford us children any *want*, unless it was Christmas, but even then, it was limited. Regardless, we always had a roof over our head, we had food on the table, and they made sure that we had *the freedom to make good choices*. This started with the best public-school education in the country. They made sure I had a lawn mower so I could cut the neighbor's lawns and a ride to Friendly's restaurant where I worked as a fountain boy scooping ice cream and as a waiter. Later on, I was a child care provider for many years.

I valued every dollar I earned and really had to measure if the wants I had were worth the hours or days it would take to earn those wants. I was responsible for paying for my own college and post-college education, so I dedicated myself to choosing an inexpensive college and took as many courses as possible so I could graduate early. I chose a major that would result in a job where I could one day support a family.

My parents succeeded in instilling in me a strong work ethic and a maturity that was unusual. They laid the foundation for me to make good decisions in life, including the value of money well-earned. They gave me a great gift – The Christian principles and virtue of discipline, self-control, and financial patience. They instilled a "pay now, play later" concept that many people today do not have. My parents instilled in me, especially through our Faith, Stewardship. They taught me not to be wasteful and to use every grace and talent for God.

Stewardship is the responsibility of God's children to use all the graces He has bestowed upon us to the best of our ability to build the Body of Christ and to return all grace for the Greater Glory of God.

That means, we need to do all we can with what we have. Some people have a lot of grace, material wealth, and good parental upbringing. Others do not. When we are standing before God, we are not judged "on the curve." Meaning, we are not judged in comparison to a single other human being. We are judged on our response to the grace we have been given. **The Lord is the Lord over our lies.** We cannot hide from Him. He knows exactly how much grace He has given us. He knows exactly what *our absolute best* is for Him with that grace or talent.

Are you a good steward of grace? Are you doing your absolute best? What is grace in your life? Let's consider five common areas of grace. Money, talent, body, relationships, and time.

Regarding finances, there seems to be a significant amount of confusion within the Catholic Church between Social Justice and Social*ism*. Although both topics are on the same spectrum of philosophy with establishing a baseline of function so one can have the freedom to make good choices; The spectrum is the difference between having a well-raised child vs. spoiled children. Catholics believe in Social Justice. Social Justice is NOT the idea that everybody has the same stuff and makes generally the same amount of money whether or not one works. It is the idea that everybody be given *the opportunity* to succeed, to have *the freedom* to make good choices.

In my own life regarding money, one good decision led to the next and then to the next. I was able to reap the rewards for this discipline and hard work. Right now, with the dawn of socialism spreading through our country like a plague, as it is pushed by the media and most universities in the country, *the freedom to make good choices is under complete and total attack.*

I have worked with the American poor for the past 30 years. The Catholic Church would never officially say the following because the Church speaks for the planet, not the USA.

I am blunt and straight forward and don't know how to speak delicately. My straightforward nature is often hailed as my greatest strength but can also be deemed as insensitive. I have struggled to find *anyone* who speaks honestly about tough topics without being labeled as insensitive. For all those who know me, they know that in my love for them, I am their most honest critic and their biggest fan.

Compared to the rest of the planet, where there is real and actual poverty, the poorest American is far richer than more than half the planet. The poorest American, through public education, an abundance of work options and resources, and a minimum wage, has at least the freedom to make good choices. In America, the poor have state sponsored food, shelter, cell phones, cable television, transportation, education, health care, air conditioning, and a retirement (social security). The poor may be more uncomfortable than others, they may not always get all of their "wants," but in Truth, they are not actually poor….. The actual poor on the planet, *despite making good choices,* are often still struggling to live.

There is no such thing as the materially poor in the United States. **The poverty of the United States is the *poverty* of *poor decision making.***

In working with the American "poor," I found that one can give them a million dollars. However, through the poverty of poor decision making, it would be spent in a month. There has been a number of studies of lottery winners that confirms this. Countless times, I have stopped to talk with and serve the homeless – They have 3 general issues. 1) Mental illness. 2) Addiction. 3) They simply do not want to work. Literally to the point where there is an argument by some for illegal immigration to perform "jobs Americans are unwilling to do."

When I went on Midnight runs to NYC to bring food to the homeless in the middle of the night, at times some of the homeless would complain about the food, the type of toothpaste being offered, or the style of clothing being offered. For some, there was little gratitude because there was often not a terrible need. How many times have we gone to the local gas station to see someone in their pajamas who rolled off the couch at 4 pm buying $15 packs of cigarettes and lotto tickets while using food stamps to buy food? Many times, we have found that those who have been given full-ride scholarships to Camp Veritas due to lack of funds, don't even show up. Given the choice, 9 times out of 10, the American poor will pick the easiest, least disciplined, wrong choice. That is why they are perpetually materially poor in a country as wealthy as ours.

To a lesser extent, these poor choices extend even to those who are working. Over 50% of the working populace of the United States has less than $1000 in the bank saved. Most are in significant credit card debt. Meanwhile, some of those I work with every day spend a ton of money to lease expensive cars, go on lavish vacations every year, go out to eat for almost all meals, waste food and utilities, and are completely incapable of saving or investing a single dollar. It is a complete exercise of the vice of Gluttony, and lack of self-control, which destroys our human dignity.

Why do these poor choices continue? They continue because too often people do not feel the pain of poor decision making. In the United States, they will still eat and have a home tomorrow, regardless of any poor decisions. In general, with our basic social network, we are already socialist to an extent. The socialism that is being pushed now is the next level that *will force us all into material slavery!*

How? Let's take the example of "Free College," which was proposed by socialists this year (2020) during our election cycle. The First Truth - NOTHING IS FREE. Anytime anybody says the word "Free," it is a lie. Somebody is paying for it. Then regarding college specifically, unlike our basic public education that is already offered, college is a luxury. Over 50% of the current positions of work in the country do not require a college education. When it is offered for "free," in essence, we will all be paying for it through our taxes which means we are still paying for it – paying the government instead of a bank for school. This will eliminate *the choice* of not going, or reaping the reward of finishing early or going to a less expensive school than others if I were to so choose. "Free" college education *enslaves* us all.

Take the college example and apply it to everything socialist and you will soon understand that **no longer will any of us have the *freedom to succeed*, the freedom to make good choices.** We will be taxed to death. The government will have complete and total control. **Socialists fear the consequences of free choice**. They do not want anybody to experience the pain involved with poor decision making. They are willing to *sacrifice the rewards of good choices,* making us all "servants of the state." A robotic people without hope of achieving anything better than the minimum. We will be like China, Cuba, and Russia, countries that are already operating like this.

Most of socialist Europe is completely bankrupt. The countries that are not bankrupt have no military as the USA continues to defend them. Most of the populace in Europe are living the religion of self, and due to socialism, few can afford children in their financial condition so their socialist model will, with mathematical certainty, fail. *There is not a single country on the planet growing in Faith in God that is Socialist.* The Government becomes God. **Socialism, with its control over our**

free-will, is a direct affront to Human Dignity, making us all dependent on Government.

Some may ask, "What does any of this have to do with religion? It sounds more political." A disclosure is that I am neither a Democrat or a Republican. Some might classify me as a Pro-Life Libertarian in identity but I don't fit into any box except Catholic.

Although Catholics strongly believe in charity, *forced charity through taxation or socialism is a type of slavery!!* **There is no grace in socialism.** When one is forced to "donate to the charity the Government chooses," there is no choice, no freedom, no act of the will. Therefore, no grace is received by the donor. When one takes through the Government's "free" hand-outs, all gratitude is replaced by entitlement, and again, no grace or humility is encountered. **Socialism eliminates free will**, and therefore eliminates love, charity, mercy, humility, gratitude, and destroys relationships with gross antagonism between those of the community.

Social economic structure has everything to do with the fruits of religious principles. **Christianity is a religion of freedom.** We are not to steal from each other, even in a vote. We are not to "covet our neighbor's goods." We are not to envy. God allows us our free will, even if it causes pain to ourselves and others. He allows us to choose Heaven and even the possibility of being separated from Him in Hell. We have the freedom to love. We have the freedom to be charitable. In that freedom, we are most in His image as sons and daughters of God.

How do Catholics reconcile that freedom, even the freedom to hoard or be selfish with Christ's demand that "If someone takes your cloak, do not withhold your tunic as well." (LK 6:30) Or how do we answer to Christ in his parable of the rich young man:

> And behold, a man came up to him, saying, "Teacher, what good deed must I do to have eternal life?" And he said to him, "Why do you ask me about what is good? There is only one who is good. If you would enter life, keep the commandments." He said to him, "Which ones?" And Jesus said, "You shall not murder, You shall not commit adultery, You shall not steal, You shall not bear false witness, Honor your father and mother, and,

You shall love your neighbor as yourself." The young man said to him, "All these I have kept. What do I still lack?" Jesus said to him, "If you would be perfect, go, sell what you possess and give to the poor, and you will have treasure in heaven; and come, follow me." When the young man heard this he went away sorrowful, for he had great possessions. Then Jesus said to His disciples, "Truly I tell you, it is difficult for a rich man to enter the kingdom of heaven. Again, I tell you, it is easier for a camel to pass through the eye of a needle than for a rich man to enter the kingdom of God." When the disciples heard this they were greatly astonished and asked, "Who then can be saved?"…(Mt 19: 16-25)

Notice, Christ did not simply tell his apostles to vote to steal the rich man's money from him. He offered the rich man the freedom to make the choice.

I am a rich man in grace, upbringing, material wealth, and talents. I am always concerned about those gifts diverting my path to Heaven. I pray that I am serving God well through those gifts so that I might make it through the "eye of needle," that I can be the steward with 10 talents.

It turns out that when we look at the lives of the saints, some of them were, in fact, financially wealthy kings or popes, yet many were poor like St. Francis. In the end, ***the attachment* to worldly goods is what we must avoid.** A saint can live the life set forth by God in peace and joy, using the 'stuff' God chooses to give or not give to him. Hoarding is not good Stewardship. Selfishness and greed are not good stewardship. The risk to the eternal soul of the rich is that the world and comfort and pleasure becomes God. It is not a sin to be a steward of many things – the sin is the attachment to those things and not being able to give up those things when the time comes to "Follow Jesus." The more one has, the tougher it is to have total and complete abandonment to those goods. Frankly, it is easier to crawl through the eye of the needle than to have that kind of abandonment. Abandonment hurts.

With monetary wealth, it is also easy to forget whose 'stuff' it is. Being a god unto oneself and forgetting that "There is a God and I am not Him" is much easier if the person is financially wealthy. It is easier for the wealthy to forget that they are dust, and that their ultimate purpose is to know and serve the Lord. It is easier to become spiritually apathetic about their dependence on God when they have no material needs. The Truth is that one does not really need many material things beyond the basics of life: food and basic housing. Beyond those basics, money has very little to do with lasting peace and joy. Those who are poor truly only own their trust in the Lord. With that simplicity comes much peace.

It reminds me of a scene in a movie called "Ironman"(2008). There is a character who is a billionaire. He is all alone in his life and he is captured by terrorists and thrown into a prison cell. In the cell with him is a poor gentleman who has a loving family which he longs to rejoin. After sharing their respective stories, the poor man ultimately tells the billionaire, "You have everything, yet you have nothing." How true that statement is for so many people across the financial spectrum.

The key with all of the blessings and graces is gratitude, acknowledging the graces we have been given in our lives. We must avoid gluttony. We are not to waste anything. We are not to use things in excess. We should care for our environment. We must then be generous in time, money, and talent...to the point *that it hurts*.

A good priest once said during Lent, "If it does not hurt, you are doing it wrong." If you are not giving to the Church, to your family, to your community, to the point where it hurts..."you are doing it wrong." We as Catholics should be investing our money generously in all areas where we give others the freedom to make good choices. This would include paying livable wages to our employees, loaning money to others for their education, financially helping the *working* poor who, again, *despite good choices,* are still struggling and seem to be penalized for working as they do not qualify for any government assistance. Love the American poor by continuing to provide them the choice of bettering their own life. Financially help those who are truly poor outside of the United States. My wife hesitates to allow me into third world countries because she knows of my deep compassion for those in true poverty, I will either adopt all of their children or give all of our money away. **It is generous to "teach others how to fish," not to just perpetually *destroy their human dignity* by indefinitely giving them fish.**

Finally, are we good stewards of our body? Our bodies are not ours. Our body is our spouses and God's. We are just a steward of it. Do we take care of the body we are giving to them? Do we offer this body to others or do we keep good stewardship in chastity? Do we concern ourselves with exercise and a healthy diet?

Other "talents" of God include how we spend our time. Do we use our time and discipline to pray, to read, to learn more about God, to volunteer, to live our vocation as a spouse or parent faithfully, to serve others, to develop human talents like art or music? Do we spend time further developing the relationships that God has given to us, especially the relationships with our family, and then the community at large? Do we mentor the youth? Do we encourage families to stay together so the teaching of a good decision-making complex is more likely to happen? Or do we use a disproportionate amount of time on our cell phones, in front of a computer or TV, or continual self-indulgence? Do we bury our talents?

Rest is fine and most needed. However, do you feel closer to God when "rest" is taking over, or do you feel spiritually sluggish…gluttonous….like we were built for something more?

Fasting is the Church's remedy to this. To combat selfishness, fast. Fast from all of those comforts in "rest" from time to time to make sure that comfort does not become our Master. Start thanking Him. Establish self-discipline and pray for an increase in virtue, especially self-control and temperance. Never spend money you don't have or can't reasonably earn. Make a five-year plan.

Take a moment from this book and start to mentally list all of those talents you have been given stewardship of by God – your Faith, your family, your talents, your time, your body, your relationships, and your material goods. **Understand that everybody is a steward of something!** Then ask yourself if you have given it all to Him, for *His* Glory or have you been using it for your glory. Are you a good Steward of the life God has given you?

Once the decision is made to serve Him in everything, when our time comes to stand before Him, like those in the parable above, you can look forward to hearing those most precious words….. "Well done my good and faithful servant, welcome home!"

Creation

For the first 14 years of my life while going to school, working, doing homework, hanging out with friends, watching TV, and living a pretty "normal life," I did not know how blind I was to the world around me. It was like I was color blind, and really had no concept that there was anything wrong. Once I found God, my eyes opened to His goodness and the tremendous gifts and graces He has given to me in my life. I was finally able to see! **One cannot love God without loving all of His Creation.**

Creation is a great gift to us. How easy it is to walk through life without stopping and appreciating this great gift! We get swept up in the fast pace and noise of life with our insatiable consumption and materialism, often taking this gift of creation for granted.

This gift of creation was given to us human beings – Those in the image and likeness of God. We were given stewardship of this creation, not to hoard or destroy this gift in our personal greed, but to live in, use for our benefit, and to replace once used in order to assure the continued availability of this God given gift for future generations.

When one loves God and their eyes are opened to Him, often, they see the world in a whole new light. From the smallest marvel of ants creating their home to the largest volcano in eruption, to birds singing to welcome the sun in the morning, to the smell of freshly cut grass or the earth after a rain, we are completely surrounded with Beauty. *Can you see Beauty?*

In our present time, in the discussion about God's Creation, we are often exposed to extremes. On one end we have those who hunt for sport to stroke their personal EGO, taking life for the sake of a trophy or amusement, while using environmental resources to their utter depletion or extinction in greed. The other extreme places so much stock in creation that they often forget that creation was given to us, not vice versa. Too often in this environmentalist extreme, they find themselves focusing all of their time and attention on saving "Mother Earth," sometimes falling into the error *of worshipping finite creation, not the infinite Creator.*

In Christianity, good stewards of God's creation are free to use this great gift of God with some parameters of consideration. First, is the resource being utilized renewable? If not, is there any other option to support Human Life? Second, if animal life is to be taken, is it done humanely and respectfully? Third, is anything from the harvesting of crops to the use of animals getting wasted? Do we try to find and utilize alternative, reusable, clean energy if possible?

When one is immersed in the beauty of God's creation, gratitude to God inevitably follows. Almost all of my prayer to God is praise and thanksgiving. It always excites me to think that **as beautiful as this Earth is, it is only a dim shadow compared to what awaits us in Heaven!**

Thank you, God for the great gift and grace you have given to us in this brief time we have here on Earth. Open our eyes so we can see you present here and now. Help us to serve you well while taking care of your creation.

Misdirected Compassion

One day, on a television show on EWTN, there was a priest in a room surrounded by several young people. These young adults were peppering the priest with question after question. The questions concerned the contemporary social "norms" about which the group thought the Church to be "out of touch." They questioned why the Church opposes gay marriage, contraception, extramarital sex, abortion, woman being priests, stem cell research, euthanasia, in vitro fertilization, missing Mass, and boyfriend/girlfriend co-habitation before marriage. These questions were intermixed with their stated opinion that the "Catholic Church has outdated views of society."

The priest stood there and absorbed what seemed like an eternity of questioning, almost like he was on the witness stand in a courtroom. The aggressive young people didn't seem to be interested in his initial answers to their questions. They continued asking the next question before he finished answering the prior question. He ultimately stopped responding to the verbal attacks, leaned back, and smiled. The commotion died down. Then the priest spoke.

"Has God Changed?" Bam! Then there was silence. These young adults got it. If God is Truth, the Truth does not change. God doesn't respond to opinion polls. The Truth doesn't change if a majority of people ignore it. The Truth doesn't change over time. *God* is the same today as He was yesterday and as He will be tomorrow. *Truth* is the same today as it was yesterday and as it will be tomorrow. **Again, there is nothing less relevant to the Truth and Reality of the universe than our personal**

opinion! Needless to say, no one in the crowd had any courage to ask him any more questions.

Most people in our society have a significant amount of compassion, which is good. We are concerned about the well-being of others. I have often commented that the *personality types* of those on the radical left and radical right of the political spectrum are nearly identical. Some simply fight more for compassion while others fight for justice and Rule of Law. These objectives are inherently good but without some balance, it is hard to exist in a functioning society.

God is Truth. Meanwhile, Satan is referred to in scripture as the "Father of Lies."(Jn8:44) At times, society *unknowingly* supports sin because we have *misdirected compassion*. We have compassion for individuals who are called to self-control and physical-mastery. That is why we don't dare to encourage people to refrain from sex until marriage. We have compassion for those with same sex attraction so we turn a blind eye to unnatural and sinful behavior. We have compassion for the woman who is choosing to terminate her child in an abortion. We have compassion for the handicapped, so if we find through ultrasound or testing that a child will be born with a handicap, we "compassionately" kill them through abortion. We have compassion for the physically ill, so we kill healthy unborn children for their cells to use in embryonic stem cell research. We have compassion for those who suffer, so we "compassionately" kill them through euthanasia. We have compassion for those confused with their sexuality so we often encourage them in their delusion. We have compassion for the poor and often fail in our duty to teach and expect basic life skills, undermining their human dignity. In the name of "compassion," Satan has slowly guided us in *justifying* the "Religion of Self" for ourselves.

Our society is missing a major rule of basic morality. **The end does NOT justify the means!** In other words, even if we could cure humanity of the horrible disease of cancer by killing only one innocent, unwilling person, it is never moral to proceed. If our end is to reduce suffering by intentionally killing those who suffer, that is never moral. If we allow a woman to "pursue happiness", but in doing so she is slaughtering her unborn children, that is never morally acceptable.

"Tolerance" of sin and evil has never been, nor should ever be, a Catholic virtue. Catholics are called to practice *charity* *to those in sin*. In the end, we are all sinners (especially me). We all have weaknesses. We all have crosses to carry. I have compassion for everyone in their weakness. That does not mean that I want to ever condone or even be apathetic to sin.

The reason why sin and evil are flourishing in our society is <u>not</u> because evil has somehow become stronger than it used to be. **It is through the apathy regarding sin by good people that sin has taken a stronghold in today's world.** Satan has caused good people to become confused. He often convinces good, holy people to avoid standing up for the Truth for fear of being hypocrites. Through this fear, Satan then acts in our society unopposed. Society then tolerates a moral code which is based upon the least common denominator of human decency.

The truth is: **we are all hypocrites!** The only non-hypocrites that have ever walked the earth are Jesus Christ and the Virgin Mary. Just because we are sinners does not mean that we should not strive to be better in mind and deed. Just because we are weak, we should not lower the "moral bar" of our society to our present state of weakness.

Likewise, we are admonished by the "politically correct" proponents, "Do not judge others!" It is true that we should not judge whether others are going to Hell. Rather, we should have mercy on all who are in error and encourage them to "sin no more." However, Satan has twisted our thinking about judging *people's souls* (predicting whether they are going to heaven or hell) versus judging an *action* as good or evil.

The result of this twisted thinking and rampant confusion is that the discernment between good and evil has become a social taboo. The Truth is: **we must judge *actions* as good or evil.** If we are aware that an action is evil and sinful due to the teaching and example of Christ, then we know it is damaging to the soul. It is like a spiritual cancer. If we love others in our society, we have a responsibility to educate them on the difference between healthy behavior and unhealthy behavior. If we know the stove is hot, we must tell others before they touch it. We cannot sit idly by and allow sin to become our cultural 'norm.' In this case, to do nothing—to be apathetic—is to sin! *True compassion* for others will lead us to show them the path to Heaven, not to sit by and idly allow sin to enslave them!

Stand up! Stand up for the Truth! Stand up for all that is good! Be a light in this time of darkness! Stand up for our Lord! Stand up for our Master! Stand up for our King!

Camp Veritas

There has always been an undercurrent of spiritual preparation and learning occurring throughout my whole life. As I entered my teen years and grew in my relationship with the Lord, I became more aware of this reality. I was being molded by the Lord. For what purpose I had yet to find out. Since then I have tried to give control of my everyday life to the Holy Spirit and in doing that, I am now convinced that **there are no accidents**. Therefore, I try to learn from every situation, whether I perceive it as good or bad, and try to identify and understand what God is trying to teach me.

The Lord is merciful. He usually only shows me the next few steps of the journey. It is like climbing a mountain in the fog. If I truly saw how large and treacherous the mountain was before I started, I probably would not have bothered trying to climb it, telling the Lord His expectations of me were impossible.

The good news is that I don't see the whole mountain; I see only the next several yards and they don't look that difficult. With that limited visibility, I find myself often doing what I would have formerly considered for me to be unlikely. For example, if you were to tell me and my English teachers in high school that I would one day be writing a book, we would have laughed out loud.

There have been many learning situations in which the Lord has taught me profound lessons. One of these lessons occurred at a point in my life when I was having a difficult time at work. I was trying to control a situation to help make our business more successful. The problem was that my warnings and suggestions were not always heeded. Following a tense meeting with my employers, I was totally stressed out. I started obsessively planning my next move: who I would talk to, what I would I say, and when would I say it. As usual, when my mind got into that obsessive problem-solving mode, I shut out everything else. I was distant to my family. I didn't sleep well. I was unable to focus on normal tasks at hand.

It was during this stressful time that my wife recommended that I attend daily Mass with her. She's so great. Gosh, I love her. I agreed. Upon arrival, we chose to sit in a front pew of church. Following Mass, a woman I had never met before approached me. I found out later that she is a Jewish convert to Catholicism. She said, "The Lord wants me to tell you something." I thought to myself, "Yeah, right lady," but I listened just to be polite. She continued, "The Lord wants you to know that He really loves you. He has great plans for you. Don't worry about it; He will take care of it." With those words, she gave me a hug and walked off.

Instantly the flood of thoughts turning the treadmill in my brain stopped. I could no longer even *think* about my work-related petty worries. I felt mental and emotional peace. Her statement became the motto of my life: **If the Lord loves me, what else *really* matters?** Everything else is anxiety about the false control I *think* I have when I forget that "**There is a God and I am not Him**." If I can look at that cross and truly believe God loves me, nothing else matters. My only remaining task is to fulfill the meaning of my life and choose to obey the Lord, moment by moment, in my life. I really do not have control over anything else. That inclination to obey flows from having the *trust* that the Lord knows what He is doing.

I continued to listen to the Lord and my next step up the mountain of life began to emerge from the fog. As I was sitting in Mass one day with my family, I looked around the church and found that we were the only people in the building under the age of 60. The mean age of the church community is rising. The youth are not retained following their Confirmation in eighth grade. The number of men answering the call to priesthood is dwindling. It is only a matter of time before churches are closed. Many churches will disappear, not in a hundred years or fifty years, but in the next ten years unless something changes. The "Religion of Self" permeates deeply within the contemporary thinking of our culture. It is destroying the individual. It is destroying the family. It is therefore destroying the Church.

As I imagined standing next to my Church while the Church seemed to be on life support from this preventable disease, my heart was broken. I love God's Church. I thought, "If I don't do something about this, how can I expect anybody else to." At the time, I thought about how I came to know the Lord. It was not by going to CCD or Confirmation class for an hour a week. It was not from some great homily I heard once in church. The way I found the Lord was by spending time with the Lord in front of the Eucharist.

One of the main reasons we are dying as a Church is because we are losing 90% of our teens the very week after they have been confirmed in the eighth grade. These teens went to their Confirmation classes weekly for years, and heard about Christ. They learned about Christ as if He were Abraham Lincoln, *yet never made the decision to actually follow him.*

A major reason for this lack of commitment is that CCD is school. Worse, it is often after a full day of actual school with sports and tests the next day immersed in all of the noise of life. As much as school regarding our Faith is necessary, it feels like detention. If Jesus was the teacher to 8th graders in this kind of environment, even He would struggle to capture these teenager's attention!

Imagine an Alcoholics Anonymous program that has meetings once a week for an hour. Imagine the alcoholics hearing about alcohol for the hour but *have never made the decision to actually stop drinking.* The first thing the alcoholic would do, would be to go home and drink following the meeting. This would continue through the entire AA program. If the Alcoholics had an AA picnic for a day, that same alcoholic would go home and drink twice as much as usual. The only thing that is effective for most alcoholics is to go to detox for a time, a time separated from their alcohol so they can make an objective choice if they want to continue with alcohol in their life or not. Only then, once the decision has been made, does the weekly meeting at AA make sense and becomes effective.

The Catholic Church has had its own detox for 2000 years. It is called pilgrimage. Pilgrimage is stepping out of our lives long enough that we can look back at our life and make the objective call of whether we are on a path that leads to our eternal destination of Heaven, or not. It is the time to make the decision to become *a disciple* of Jesus Christ. Only after that decision is made, does going to Mass make sense. Only then does going to Confirmation class make sense to continue to nurture that decision.

As a chubby boy at heart, I think of many things in relation to food. Imagine the Church has great barbeque sauce. Imagine the sauce is made up of the Mass, Adoration, the rosary, catechesis, and personal testimonies. Then imagine dumping that sauce all at once on some ribs. The sauce all burns off. It does not soak in. Imagine microwaving the ribs. They taste just awful. The key to good cooking in this case is time. **The key ingredient to making disciples of Christ, is time in front of the Cross – time in front of the Eucharist.** There is nothing wrong with the recipe the Church has been using for millennia. Those running these programs have simply turned up the heat too much and the sauce is burning off. We are trying to teach the entirety of the church in some 6-hour retreat. It is simply not enough time to have these youth step out of the busyness of their lives to listen. It is not enough time in front of the Cross to allow the reality of the Cross to soak in and build a personal relationship with God.

Allowing the grace of the Cross to soak in also entails identifying the enemy: the "Religion of Self." It is much easier to fight a disease when you identify what the disease is. Through prayer, and finally submitting to the persistent nagging of my heart by the Lord, the solution became obvious. Stamp out the "Religion of Self"; introduce teens to their God; and invite them to drink the living water of grace found at the base of the Cross. Invite them to drink not just little sips, but to dive head-first into that font of grace!

This is where the idea of Camp Veritas came to fruition (Veritas in Latin means "Truth"). Camp Veritas would be an overnight camp where the youth of the Faith stop the busyness of their lives for a week and go on pilgrimage to be with the Lord. Camp Veritas would offer education about the Faith.

I found that in some parishes, the teens are taught by volunteers that are usually not comfortable teaching teens. They are often broken down into "small groups" where the teen's opinion is solicited about how they 'feel' about the teaching of the Church. This only encourages the "Religion of Self" within the Faith as it fosters a delusion that the teen's opinion actually matters to the Reality of the universe. Furthermore, there is inconsistency with what is being taught about the Faith. And frankly, some of these volunteers, God bless them and their willingness to serve, are not very good at it. I found that a good teacher is as effective teaching 10 teens as that same teacher would be teaching 1000. Why would we not allow our youth to be taught by the very best teachers of our Faith? Why not have those who teach youth for a living and are comfortable with it, teach the masses. Camp Veritas could then be the one place a parish would know their kids are being taught by the best teachers that the Catholic Church has to offer and taught the Faith consistent with our teaching authority of Rome.

Camp Veritas would teach the kids how to pray. Most simply do not know how. They have never been exposed to prayer. Camp would fill them with grace through Confession and the reception of the Eucharist, and introduce them to a vibrant community of believers, including priests and other religious.

The key to this experience is to introduce the teens to the Lord at a rate that is tolerable. Pouring knowledge of the Truth onto a teen when their glass is already overflowing is not useful or fun. The average human being has about 45 min of attention before they cannot compute any more information at that time. Jesus Himself had to do a miracle every 45 minutes to keep the people's attention. At Camp Veritas, although we are not usually breaking up instruction with walking on water, healing the blind and the lame... we have laser tag, swimming pools, climbing walls, and talents shows. We have great entertainment in between the religious instruction so the teens do not feel like they are in class all day. This allows the teaching moments to soak in. This means Camp Veritas could be held anywhere the teens can eat, sleep, be taught, and entertained for a week. In short, the objective of the week would be to play and pray and activate in each young Catholic camper the desire to reevaluate their life priorities by questioning where they came from and where they are going, and continue *in the Lord* one step at a time up the mountain of life.

My initial approach was to propose the idea to Cardinal Egan—the man at the top at the time - reiterating the concept of Camp Veritas. Much to my disappointment, Cardinal Egan himself wrote me a letter essentially stating, "Good luck. I will pray for YOU as you begin your camp." My reaction was, "great, now what? What do I know about beginning and leading a camp? What do I know about leading youth? Who would come to a camp run by the random guy named Ryan Young anyway? What kind of credibility do I have? Where, in all my education regarding medicine, have I ever been taught these skills? I did not even go to camp as a kid. Has the Lord lost His mind?"

Also, it quickly became apparent to me that starting a camp would entail a lot of time and money. It would detract from my family responsibilities. I was being called into a service that would entail a great sacrifice of my time which would challenge my call as husband and father. Like any man who goes to war, I was a man being called into the battle of souls. **I had to be willing to sacrifice the time I might spend with my family so at some point, my children can live in a much better world.**

My saving grace is that my wife has always been onboard. She has the same priorities in her life that I have in mine. Our priority is Heaven. It is through this reality that she feels called to "hold down the fort". Her attitude allows me to then "go forth." I have been truly blessed to have a wife that understands the big picture; she is like the supply train to the battlefield for souls.

The Lord was showing me the first few steps of the "mountain in the fog," so I started climbing. After all, if *I* do not act, who will? I started this climb up this mountain with the foundation of who I am; I began by presenting the idea of Camp Veritas to my immediate family. After all, they are the most Catholic people I know. These are God's saints. My family is full of holy, talented, and intelligent people who love the Church. They are not blind to the bleak future of our Church in our region if nothing changes. The reaction I received from those I love most was surprising. My parents and most my siblings shook their heads and laughed and told me that an idea of this magnitude could not be done. I was told it was "unrealistic" and the problems we face in our Church were simply "too big."

My older brother, who has been a great example of faith to me in my life and is one of my Heroes, relayed his personal experience with trying to renew our Faith. A year earlier, he tried to start a prayer group for his parish. He invited hundreds of young adults to his parish for their opening meeting. Flyers were placed at numerous local parishes. My brother wanted to order fifteen pizzas for the crowd he was expecting. To his dismay, his parish priest ordered three pizzas and told my brother he would order more if needed. Needless to say, 3 people showed up. Those three people were my brother and our siblings. My brother's conclusion was that the Church was already dead in our region and beyond life-support.

My older sister whose conversion was the catalyst of my family's conversion in the Faith, who attends daily mass and home-schools her eight saintly children, did not believe teenagers would ever willingly attend this camp, much less convince their parents to pay a fee for them to attend. She brought up the numerous logistical challenges I would face in opening a camp, such as adult volunteer supervision, need for lifeguards, entertainment, difficulty with weather, and so forth. As she spoke, the mountain of this task the Lord placed in front of me was unveiled. This mountain was enormous. The journey ahead seemed hard, practically impossible. That moment reminds me of when Peter tried to convince Jesus not to enter Jerusalem where He would be crucified and "At this he turned around and, looking at his disciples, rebuked Peter and said, 'Get behind me Satan. You are thinking not as God does, but as human beings do.'" (Mk 8:33)

My younger sister is one of the most holy people I know. Not only did she think the idea of this Camp was too big; she especially thought the idea was too big for me. The problem I was facing with my family is that they know me the most. They know of my many weaknesses. They know the road I have traveled. She had no faith in *me*. What she didn't realize is that I do not have faith in *me* either. I am nothing in the grand scheme of things. Who am I to even attempt something as crazy as Camp Veritas? She believed I was having delusions of grandeur. Although I don't believe I am a prophet, it reminds me of Jesus saying, "Amen, I say to you, no prophet is accepted in his own native place."(Lk 4:24) My immediate family, who is religious, did not believe in this idea. Considering the poor state the Church is in, what would the rest of the Church family think?

Ironically, the only person in my immediate family who thought the idea of Camp Veritas had any value and didn't shoot the idea down outright was my youngest sister (the same sister who finally attended Mass after the fly repeated landed on her face.) Go figure?

The truth is that my family was right. All of their objections and concerns were completely valid. I did not have any answers for them. In fact, I agreed with all of their objections. I thought the Lord was crazy for asking me to start a camp. But that was the point. The only thing I really knew for certain was that the Lord was asking me to do this. I had faith in that call of the heart. I had faith without understanding. Although I felt completely alone at that moment, although the mountain looked too big for me to climb, the only response I could give to my family was, **"I told the Lord I would try to answer His call and that I would give my absolute best, so I intend on doing so."**

The next few steps of the "mountain in the fog" emerged and I climbed further. I spent most of my "free time" for a year getting the camp off the ground. I was forced to do things like call strangers. As an introvert, I would first develop a cold sweat and get nauseated as I paced around the phone. Then I would say to myself, "For your Glory Lord," pick up the phone and dial before I could change my mind. I would make a call to someone I thought could help, and they would advise me to call someone else to cover other aspects of logistics and so forth. The Holy Spirit took me step by step because I had no idea what I was doing. I was a man on a mission and I would not take "no" for an answer. **"No" was not a possibility to me. I was on a mission from God. The only thing that mattered was how I was to get to "yes."** Ultimately, after a year's worth of efforts and promotion, and with the help of my father behind the scenes, handling all of the processes of establishing a non-profit corporation, the pieces of Camp Veritas quickly fell into place and the Camp was ready to receive camper enrollments.

I have generally been successful in my worldly endeavors throughout my whole life. I have always done well in school, work, finances and so forth. I 'succeeded' at most things I attempted. With regards to the camp, the number of enrollments compared to my expectations was pathetic. We were not even close to reaching the minimum number of campers that we had negotiated in our contract with the camp facility we planned to rent for the week. This was like the prayer-group pizza party my brother had thrown for his parish, however multiplying that disaster times 100. I felt like the Ark had been built, it was raining heavily, but nobody was getting into the boat. I was embarrassed for our Church. I really did not know how to explain to the camp facility how the entire Catholic Church in our region only had about 12 teens willing to come. Frankly, it was a really distressing time.

In the worldly sense, I had failed. I had tried my very best and I had failed. I was ready to give up and cancel the project. It was at this moment of decision, lying in bed late one night, that I prayed to God in relative despair. I told Him in prayer, "I am so sorry. I tried my absolute best and completely failed..... I am so sorry."

Much to my surprise, the biggest "burning bush" moment of my life thus far occurred right then. He then gave me a dramatic vision like a movie screen going off in my mind. Tens of thousands of people – beyond count - dropping to their knees in front of the Eucharist, over and over and over...everywhere. I would become the *"Father of thousands!"* He asked me in my mind, "Ryan, who's time was it? Yours Lord. Whose money is it? Yours Lord. Whose life is it? My life is yours Lord. "Whose camp is this? It is yours Lord."

Immediately I had absolute peace. This was God's project and thus His problem. Like the story of Gideon (Jg 7), God wanted to make sure I knew this camp did not exist due to my efforts. **There is no such thing as failure in attempting to do the will of the Lord because, in obeying Him—in taking those steps up that mountain—***I have already won!* God never guaranteed *worldly* success. He did, however, promise to provide me with peace and joy if I obeyed, and ultimately, on that front, He came through.

Our youth could attend camp as the norm for their Catholic upbringing in their immediate pre and post Confirmation time. They would take spiritual tools from camp that could be applied in their home, their church, and their community for years to come. They would take the spiritual fire they received from the camp and use it to expel the darkness they encountered in our culture. Thousands of adults would join them in this great battle for the soul. They would participate in the transfiguration of the "Mystical Body of Christ." They would participate in the revolution against the "Religion of Self."

As I saw this vision in my mind, I literally laughed out loud. The thought of national expansion was the single most ridiculous thought I have ever had up to this point in my life, especially when only a dozen teens signed up after a year of effort. *It was so ridiculous that it could have only been from Him.* I felt like the elderly, childless Sarah when God assured her husband Abraham that "you will have descendants as numerous as the stars."(Gen22:17) I was so incredulous that I told God that He had better get going given that our Camp Veritas situation did not look very good.

The next day, I met with my local bishop and he encouraged me to persist, so I went back to my journey and took another step up the mountain.

Ultimately, many members of my family got on board with the idea of Camp Veritas and started to help out. With their efforts, over 50 youth attended the first year. The recipe of Camp Veritas was now tested and perfected. We were delighted that the kids got so much out of it. Prior to our first camp, I received a warning call from a mother telling me she was sending her very resistant 17-year-old son to camp. On the last day of camp this same teen said, "You saved a lot of souls this week, including my own." Two years later, as Cardinal Timothy Dolan's van drove into camp, that same former camper jumped out of the van as a seminarian.

Meeting Cardinal Dolan at Camp Veritas many years ago was somewhat surreal. As I gave him a tour of the facility, I told him of the vision of "franchising" the Camp Veritas recipe and taking it everywhere. If it worked in New York, why would the same recipe not work in Chicago, Los Angeles, Denver, Miami, St. Louis, or Seattle? Unlike so many times before with so many other people, he listened and did not look at me like I was totally crazy. After he heard the plan, he looked at me with a wry smile and stated, "How far are you willing to go?" I answered, "How much is a soul worth?" Every day, as I awake to this battle for souls, those words ring out to me, **"How far are you willing to go, Ryan? How much is a soul worth?"**

As I have had the honor of getting to know Cardinal Dolan a bit over the years, and after seeing how filled he is with the Holy Spirit, I am no longer laughing incredulously at God any longer. With his help and with the help of my family and many other Saints of God, Camp Veritas is expanding rapidly. We are approaching our 11th year and now have 1500 enrollments with over 500 volunteer support staff and religious, divided into 5 camps, including a camp in Ireland yet this is still just the beginning.

God directly helps a number of our departments for Camp Veritas, including staffing. I have the handicap of struggling with most people's names and I live a reasonably private life. I know very few people. Yet every year, at every camp (and there has been more than 30 camps) there are the exact number of male volunteer chaperones to boys in attendance and female volunteer chaperones proportionate to the girls in attendance.

God has called them all by name and the precise number of volunteers show up. That is a miracle.

God does not allow for a straight path up this mountain in the fog. As I mentioned earlier, God never draws in straight lines. Rather he scribbles like a 2-year-old having me go up, then down, then left, than down further, before we go up again.... Each step picking up more of the "willing" who are joining me with this journey up the mountain for souls. These adults have inspired me. Their "yes" inspires the "yes" of so many others. So many people have found God through this great gift of Camp Veritas. Perhaps in reading this book, you would like to join us in this most important, eternally life changing endeavor. I have found that at times with God, **the goal is not always about the destination, but sometimes the victory is in the journey!**

I learned through this experience to be at peace with God's plan and give up control. I learned that the Lord will use me in ways I would not have expected. I learned not to put limits on the Lord and to stop guessing how long and difficult the journey will be up the mountain of my life. I learned to have faith and trust in the Lord. I learned how to properly measure success in my life. **I learned that nothing is impossible with God!**

The Camp Veritas portion of my journey up the mountain of life continues for me, my family, the campers, the adult volunteers, the dedicated priests, religious sisters and friars, and the camper's parents. If you have an interest in learning more about the camp—the boot camp for souls—please check us out at www.campveritas.com.

If I Were Satan

Enjoy reading this unedited chapter that I originally wrote 8 years ago which turned out to be quite prophetic....

I grew up playing chess. The key to playing chess well is to anticipate your opponent's next move and act accordingly. I have a singular remaining mission in my life: That is to bring as many eternal souls that I possibly can to the foot of the Cross and allow the Lord to do the rest. That mission has become an obsession of sorts. I have found that it influences every decision I make every day. It is the reason I am writing this book, at this very moment.

Satan also has a singular objective. His only mission is to draw us away from the Cross. He uses the dust of the world to do so. He is a cunning adversary and the moment we let up our guard to him is the moment he has already won.

The following thoughts are my thoughts. These thoughts are simply what I would do if I were Satan. These are not necessarily the teaching of the Catholic Church.

As I have already died to myself, I have nothing left to lose. What is Satan going to do to me? Kill me twice? With that freedom, I have been able to run about the battlefield and assess the situation. Right now, it is like Satan is on a hill, lobbing mortar fire on our entrenched positions. We, the Church, have been hiding defensively in our bunkers for decades, hoping he won't aim at us next. For many, the bunkers have become entirely too comfortable. Slowly but surely, Satan is taking out our positions, one school, one hospital, and one church at a time.

He has amassed an army that is presently on the move at high speed due to our new digital age. As he seems to be working through the internet, the Catholic Church still seems to be using the pony express. Satan is succeeding because of several tactics. First, as already discussed throughout this book, corrupt the souls of all through the "Religion of Self." Next, if I were Satan, I would control information. Control TV, the radio, movies, education, and print literature. Most media is printing and speaking half-truths or flat lies and the rest is spreading fear, all of which is not of God. Satan frames all Truth in his agenda, twisting that Truth slowly enough that from moment to moment, we are unaware of how far we have turned from the Lord.

Recently, after flipping through 200 channels, my wife stated, "Where have all of the men gone?" The guys on TV are either stupid, act like a bunch of pre-pubescent boys or college partying idiots, or are prancing around the TV as if they are women. When is the last time you have seen a strong, upright, confident man sacrificing himself for anything other than self on TV? The last time I can remember seeing a normal, traditional family on TV was the Cosby Show, Little House on the Prairie, or Family Ties in the 1980's. There is EWTN, the Catholic channel. It is nicely tucked away on channel 97 within an ocean of other channels. Out of sight, out of mind.

Who is Catholic on TV that accurately teaches or stands for the teaching of our Catholic Church? Bishop Fulton Sheen used to be that face in the 1950's. Now, the only 'Catholics' we are exposed to publicly are those that are in blatant opposition and even scandal against the Church, especially regarding issues of life. These include Lawrence O'Donnell, Rachel Maddow, and Chris Mathews on MSNBC, Chris Cuomo on CNN, or leading politicians with great influence like Nancy Pelosi, Joe Biden, John Kerry, Andrew Cuomo, and Rudy Giuliani. If I were Satan, I would encourage that "scandal" (open opposition to the Catholic Church while proclaiming to be a Catholic themselves) to run amuck so to be "Catholic" really doesn't mean anything because all the "Catholics" we ever publicly see seem to believe in what they please, not serving a Truth larger than themself. They clearly seem to value their political worldly success and affiliation more than their identity as Catholic.

If I were Satan, and I wanted to control information, I would control schools. I would put an emphasis on the good of public education in a community; such an emphasis that the populous would feel compelled through misdirected compassion to *pay anything* for it. The disproportionate cost of public schools would then create a tax culture where although we are "free" to have a Catholic education, after paying our public-school taxes, nobody can afford to go to a catholic school. After a while, I would make it illegal to home-school children, as of course the government could educate our kids better than our parents can, so it would be child-abuse to not put our children in public school, right?

If I were Satan, I would emphasize the beauty of God's creation of our planet and environment so much, that it would encourage people to fall in love with creation rather than the Creator. I would create a culture where having children would actually be viewed as selfish, as children might require resources and might therefore be harmful to "mother earth" so out of compassion to mother earth, laws would be construed to limit the number of children we have. China's present 1 child only per family while the rest are slaughtered through abortion would be the next logical step.

If I were Satan, I would slowly force the populous to participate in sin. This would foster an attitude where because we are already forced to sin, what is just one more? We already pay for abortion as tax payers in this country indirectly. We subsidize Planned Parenthood with our tax dollars which pays for the building where abortions are performed, the abortion "doctor's" salaries, the heat, overhead, and equipment. If that is the case, out of "compassion" for "woman's health," why not force Catholic institutions and employers to directly pay for early abortion-causing drugs for their staff? Note that the media intentionally and repeatedly calls these drugs "contraception," not the "morning after pills" that many of these truly represent.

If I were Satan, I would attack the Catholic Church's freedom of speech. I would make sin legal, like "gay marriage," so if the Church was to speak out against this *sin*, it would be construed as "hate speech," discrimination, or bigotry. Right now, in England, yes I did not say Syria or China, I said England; a woman lost her job because she wore a small cross to work. If I were Satan, I would classify all discussion about faith, the "imposing" of religion on others and eventually remove all discussion about God from everywhere unless one wanted to risk fines or imprisonment. This, of course would be out of "compassion" for unbelievers.

If I were Satan, I would encourage dependence of a populace on government, not God. For millennia, the Catholic Church has been the staple in culture to serve the infirmed and educate the poor. The Church was able to freely contribute its 2000 years of knowledge and wisdom through its service to society. The Catholic Church *invented* the University, the Hospital, and organized charity. This was supported financially through the *voluntary* charity of those in the pew, the "Body of Christ."

If I were Satan, I would use our rightful compassion to the infirmed, the aged, children, and the handicapped and then push to extend that compassion to the 'takers' of our society. Working in health care, I am exposed daily to those who are completely able-bodied, taking advantage of the *forced* charity of others through governmental subsidy. I deal with numerous "disabled" people who can still drive, talk, walk, and go bowling. It is not that these individuals can't work, they simply choose not to. Through "Misdirected Compassion," they take from the government free education, housing, food, health care, transportation, cable television, air-conditioning, retirement, and a cell phone. Why work? The amount of 'takers' has become an epidemic. I am often exposed to people who seem to have enough money for expensive hair styling, designer clothing, manicures, and cigarettes yet these same individuals claim they do not have enough money for the $10 copay of their own child's medicine.

Forced charity (another term for slavery) through tax, removes all grace from charity. By forcefully taking money from those who are working, because that person did not freely give that money away, he does not receive grace. He does not take any step toward the objective of Heaven. Those who are taking that money to remain "disabled," or purposely unemployed, grow in a sense of entitlement, not gratitude, and therefore the recipient of those funds does not receive grace either. "When we were with you, we instructed you that if anyone was unwilling to work, neither should that one eat." (2Th3:10). Christ did not tell his apostles to *force* the rich man to give away his goods to the poor. Christ *invites us* to make that choice.

A Catholic is to fight that everybody in a society has the *opportunity*, the *freedom*, to make good choices and have the ability to labor for a just wage. A Catholic is not obligated to perpetually enable sloth and dependence. A Catholic is not obligated to perpetually bail out those making bad decisions. God, through love, has given us the ability to make decisions, some good and some bad. He allows us to experience the consequences of those decisions, good and bad. In other words, if a Catholic truly loves his brother, instead of fostering dependence by perpetually giving the "hungry" fish, the Catholic would instead teach the hungry to fish themselves, fostering freedom from dependence. **Otherwise, forming people to be chronically dependent on others is an affront to human dignity.**

A Catholic would also care for those who are vulnerable, those who have no ability to physically contribute to the community such as the very old, very young, mentally handicapped, or the very sick as we understand the value of human dignity because the breath of God is in them.

If I were Satan, I would encourage economic dependence on government, removing the freedom of a populace to exercise free-will, creating a form of slavery. Just ask anyone who has fled Russia, East Berlin, North Korea, and China how the government ultimately becomes the people's 'god.' Ask then how free they were to believe in the true God of the Universe. Ask how free the Catholic Church was in serving the community in those countries. Can you think of one Socialistic or Communist Country where the Catholic Church is presently growing? A government that wants to be 'god' usually does not like competitors.

If I were Satan, I would do everything I could to promote Islamic violent extremism. Pope Benedict the XVI was right when he noted, "How true can a faith be if one needs a gun to promote it?" As the world goes to war with Islamic violent extremism, is it so hard to imagine this war of violence spreading onto religion itself, including Christianity? Satan does not care about politics. He does not care about maps. He cares only for souls.

If I was Satan, I would attack the priesthood with everything I got. Take down the shepherd, you scatter the sheep. I would dig up every scandal I possibly could in the Church over the past 50 years. Every time the Catholic Church is discussed, I would somehow incorporate the word "scandal" in the same article. I would want to destroy the credibility of the Church to the population it serves.

If I were Satan, I would cause as much division as I could within the Church itself. I would encourage, through pride, many religious to disregard their authority in Rome. I would encourage "pluralism" and "tolerance" to the point where heresy would be accepted as merely another point of view; where there was no longer a memory of the objective Truth of Jesus Christ or his teaching authority in the Magisterium.

If I were Satan, I would paint the Catholic Church as a non-compassionate, scandal ridden entity of old men who are out of date with an "enlightened" world. I would paint the Catholic Church as sexist, bigoted, intolerant, and did I already mention, non-compassionate? Do not the points of this chapter seem familiar to us all? Have we not all seen this organized, systematic attack from Satan spreading throughout our land like a tsunami that is wiping out all that is good? How long are we going to stay down, hiding in our bunker? *How many souls are we willing to lose* while we wait around, hoping that some other person acts as Christ's voice, hands, and feet?!

No more...NO MORE!! It is time to charge the hill! I have breath right now. You have breath right now. If we do not act, who will? If now is not the time to act, then when? Once there is no one left? In Christ, *we* are the hope of the future in this world! We have the opportunity to face these forces of darkness head on. The Truth of our Faith should never be in retreat. We should never operate in fear! **One hour of Truth dispels years of lies.** Even the smallest light in Truth is bright in the darkness. We should never go away! We should never go quietly into the night! We are Disciples of Jesus Christ that need to stand as one and charge Satan's position on that hill together. In doing so, we can and will win this war for souls. Christ, through the Cross has already given us the victory! We now, through our voices and talents in love, have the opportunity to bring this victory to the world as the "Good News." We must bring to all people of the world the light of His victory! **How far are you willing to go? How much is a soul worth? Answer the call! Answer the call! And together in Christ, we will change the world!!**

Discipleship

All right Ryan. I just finished reading the last chapter. Although I think you should consider taking some valium, I am inspired to go out and save the world from itself! Now what?...**BE YOURSELF!** God has made you a unique, one of a kind, masterpiece! There has never been, nor will there ever be, anyone in the history of world just like you. God made you with specific talents and unique abilities. All He asks of us is that we offer the only thing we have the power to offer; to give our will to Him. In giving Him our will, we are giving Him our talents and gifts and ultimately our lives.

Missionary discipleship is *purposeful* discipleship. It has been misunderstood as having to go somewhere. Most people think that being a missionary means you must travel to Central America or Africa and preach the life of Christ for a week or perform community service.

Certainly, I do not want those traveling on missions to feel like they are wasting time. Mission trips are great endeavors to grow closer to God and to some extent, these trips are a pilgrimage. Missionary trips are often an answer to the prayer of those needing help, and as discussed in the chapter on Stewardship, a great way to spend our material resources.

Realistically, although the mission materially benefits those who are being served, it is difficult to establish life-long relationships with the populace because there is not enough time. Those trips serve more to build deeper relationships with God than to necessarily build relationships with people thousands of miles away.

Missionary discipleship is not a destination. IT IS A STATE OF BEING. It is not the call of a missionary – it is the call of every Catholic, every follower of Jesus Christ, our Master. Christ sent His followers out with the command to make disciples. He did not just leave them in the "upper room."

Where is the mission? Let God show you. It is right in front of your face, most of the time. First, your family. Second, your co-workers. Everybody God puts into your path. **Our job is to go fishing for souls.** We do this by recognizing that every interaction we have with every individual we encounter all day is not an accident. That every conversation that we have with others or moments we have to serve others is to imagine that Jesus Christ Himself is the other individual that we are speaking to, interacting with, serving, and choosing to love.

Our families are the people that we love the most, and that often drive us the craziest. Often, our greatest human victories and our greatest failures derive from how good of a son or daughter, brother or sister, and parent that we are. Our biggest wounds most often come from our family, as those are the people with which we allow ourselves to be vulnerable. God has given us our families to form us in virtue. It is in the family that we are "schooled" in patience, self-sacrifice, kindness, and all other virtue. The family is the bridge between God and "our neighbor." It is the Domestic Church and the fundamental building block of society. Without the family, there is no society.

To love them means to be there for them, to seek to communicate with them, and to be able to continue communicating and supporting them even if we need to disagree with them or disagree with a life-choice they've made. Although we should love our family, we should not be blind to unhealthy family dynamics. Part of our family's purpose is to push us to be better than we would be on our own. We must be aware of ways that our family is authentically dysfunctional - no family is perfect.

Our love for Christ must be stronger than our love for our family, as He says, "Anyone who loves their father or mother more than me, is not worthy of me. Anyone who loves their son or daughter more than me, is not worthy of me." (Mt 10:37) Our *ultimate* family is the Church, where we will always find a home and love.

The key to fishing for souls is to first love and exist in a state of Peace and Joy, otherwise your words or life example will mean nothing. **Only after the fish *know* without doubt that you love them, will they be**

willing to "be caught" by the Truth. Don't force it. Love, love, love, love, love and *the fish will come to you with questions and openness to the Truth*. If we are living within the Truth, it should not be a hard sell.

The next step is to reel them in once they bite. Do not be weak in the Faith or Truth. Do not compromise in the Truth. The biggest mistake of the missionary is to think that they must seem to agree with everybody all the time or water down the Truth in order to be accepted. That is a great lie! Those who agree with everybody all of the time in all things may be perceived as "nice," but are by definition, disingenuous and weak. Meet people where they are with the Truth that they can handle at that moment, but make sure that the Truth is the Truth. The only reason they are willing to "be caught" is that people want something more than what they already have.

Pope Francis, upon his first interviews with the media, was bombarded with the same 6 questions that they ask of every pope, every time they speak to him. "Why can't we have extra marital sex?" "What is wrong with Euthanasia?" "Why can't we have abortions?" "What is wrong with homosexuality?" "What is wrong with contraception?" "What is wrong with women becoming priests?"

The pope's answer was, "I will never answer those questions again. My predecessors have already answered those same questions over the past 30 years. Listen to them. Let's start talking about Jesus Christ."

Pope Francis understands that focusing on and the teaching of contemporary issues is the distant branch of the tree of Truth. He understands that if you do not know Jesus Christ, who is the root of the tree and the trunk, no answer would make sense to those in the darkness. Instead, he does not waste time in the branches. He invites all to level 1 in the Faith with Christ. Level 37 of the Catholic Faith becomes self-evident once one starts walking on the path of Truth and sacrificial love.

Don't be afraid to get uncomfortable!! Invite all to a relationship with Christ. Don't miss the opportunity for that soul once they bite, which may never come around again. Invite them in. Sacrifice your time. Be patient. How much is an eternal soul worth? The risk of losing friendship, being rejected, humiliated, or shunned is worth the reward of eternal life for yourself and them. They have a free will that will either recognize and absorb the Truth, or reject it. Your job is to throw out the seed of Truth *in love*.

How do we become missionary disciples? We must prepare and receive the sacraments. Read religious books like the Catholic Catechism or books from the saints. Especially read the Scriptures. Pray. You cannot give what you do not have. However, that is just the beginning. You must decide to die to yourself. Then you must decide to leave the upper room.

Decide that your name as Catholic means something. When my children are acting like imbeciles, I remind them that they are my children. I remind them that our name means something. I remind them that they are royal. I would explain that the name "Catholic" through our Baptism is by definition royal! "Christians, remember your dignity!" (Pope St. Leo the Great) We must always behave as dignified, confident, loved, children of God, both in our interactions with others in person and on the internet. We must live up to our name! Our name is precious and if we choose to be in the Catholic family, we should strive to bear that name with honor.

If your life as a Catholic ends with Mass once a week, you are failing as a Disciple of Jesus Christ!! We are a missionary Church! By definition, if you claim to be a Catholic, you are a missionary! It is not somebody else's job!

How do you rate your success? Do not worry yourself in the reaction of those around you when they are exposed to the Truth. *Christ Himself could not convert everybody*, including the Pharisees and Sadducees. He literally healed the blind man within feet of the Pharisees and Sadducees, and rather than seeing God 3 feet away, they could only see a man who healed on the sabbath day. They were blind to the Truth itself. Their hearts were hard. "With slabs, thicker than the stone closing the entrance of a sepulchre, has it placed on the sight of its soul not to see this Light. What mountains of sins has it on itself to be so oppressed, separated, blinded, deafened, chained, paralyzed as to stand *inert* before the Savior?" (Valtorta)

Your test is not whether you convert a single person. That is God's job. Your test is only your "yes." To exist in and speak the Truth, especially when the opportunity arises. Your test is to throw out as much seed of Truth that you can. In doing that, you have already won the race! As I said before, God does not grade on the curve. He only judges our best.

One of the greatest obstacles of discipleship is that people claim that they do not have time. If that is the case, perhaps eternal life is not as high on the priority list that it should be. If you are too busy, perhaps you are just too busy. **If you are a Catholic and *are comfortable*, then by definition, "you are doing it wrong!" Get uncomfortable! Nothing is more important than the soul.**

In trying to discern what God wanted me to do with my life, I needed to first identify *who I am*. Most people of the world identify themselves as what they do or what they are good at. I used to identify myself as a student, a musician, an athlete, and a member of my family. Then at some point, my most basic identity dawned on me. **Through my Baptism, I am a Prince. I am heir to the Kingdom of Heaven. I am a disciple of Jesus Christ.** Nothing else I do in this world is more important than that reality. When the world identifies me as crazy or "unenlightened," I answer, "Perhaps I am, but I am a Prince and heir to the Kingdom of Heaven. I am a disciple of Jesus Christ so who cares how *you* want to identify me?" **I know who I am**.

I am no longer defined by the world. God Himself paid the price at the Cross *for me*. It is He who identifies me as one of His children. It is He that established my value. Through my new identity in Christ, it is not like I am just hanging around, expecting God to rain manna down from the sky on me. I have taken my true identity in Christ and super infused that identity on the rest of my being. With that new identity, I live what most would classify as a very ordinary life. I still do everything I used to do; I just do it for a different reason: with the identity of Christ. Living with the identity of Christ, my life is anything but ordinary. I have purpose and meaning, even while doing the dishes. I have joy, even when just cutting the lawn. I have peace in the simple things: a sunset, watching the kids play and laugh, hearing the cows next door moo, feeling the breeze on my face, and listening to the rain. My identity in Him has changed everything about me.

In giving up our lives to Him and allowing Him to be our Master, there is peace and joy in everything we do. Although our lives may seem very 'ordinary' to most, when we are living our lives for the Lord, whether we are teachers or housekeepers or doctors, there is nothing 'ordinary' about our lives. We have purpose. We have reason for our being. We have life. We have freedom.

"We must become aware that God dwells in us and as we do everything for Him, that we are never commonplace, even when performing the most ordinary task. For we do not live in these things, we go beyond them. A supernatural soul never deals with natural causes but with God alone." (St. Elizabeth of the Trinity)

What the Lord asks of me is that I use the talents and gifts He gave me for *His* glory, not for mine. He built me with the intelligence and personality to work in health care, so I am a Physician Assistant for His glory. He has called me to be a husband and father. I have, therefore, been married for over twenty years and have eight children for His glory. He has given me the talent of singing; therefore, I cantor at my church for His glory. He has given me the ability to speak; therefore, I minister to all who are open to hearing the Truth, and many who are not. He has given me the ability to teach, so I am writing this book. I must always remind myself that in all that I do, in all that I achieve, I am nothing but dust, as are my 'accomplishments.' The major difference with my new identity in Christ is my choice to now live for God's glory and not for my own.

God has given each of us a myriad of talents and abilities. He will use us uniquely as we are created uniquely. The "Body of Christ" has many parts. Although the parts are different, they are all special and important. My path up the mountain is likely to be somewhat different than yours because we are different parts of this one, living body. We are uniquely made. We are the salt of the Earth! (Mt 5:13)

God has built some of us to be professional athletes, so be the best athlete you can be for the glory of God. He has built others to stay at home and raise children; so raise the greatest, holiest children for the glory of God. He has built others to be investment bankers; so be a great banker for the glory of God. God has built others to be garbage collectors; so be the best garbage collector this world has ever seen for His glory. God has built others to become priests; thank you, Lord, for these holy men. No matter what our talents, no matter what our station in life or how much money we have, we have the chance to stand out as an example to others and give God glory. Wherever this journey with the Lord leads us, we have a chance to be a light in the darkness. We need to be active in our Church. We need to be active in our culture. We need to be the voice of authority, the voice of light, Truth, and beacon to draw all souls out of the world of illusion to the world of Reality.

God has a plan for you. Isn't that a cool thought? God has an adventure in store *for you* from this point forward, an adventure that will have you climbing higher on the 'mountain of life' than you had ever dreamed possible. He has an adventure planned for you whereby He will expand the capacity of your very being in every aspect of your life. He is calling *you* to shine like the sun. He is ready to tap *your* incredible potential. *You* are called to be the greatest saint this world has ever seen. Find your identity in Christ! Walk with the Lord on this journey! Never stray from His side! Never lose hope! Never forget about the finish line!

I pray that the Lord will mold us into His image. I pray for the grace to do His will. I pray that we will all have the courage to reach up and take His hand and allow Him to lead us in this first step up our personal mountain of life to His Glory forever and ever! Amen.

Epilogue

To my children:

Kids, I really cannot express into words how much I love you and how proud I am of the saints of God that you are becoming. It has been the greatest gift and honor of my life to have been your father. Continue to live lives worthy of your name and identity as "Children of God." I look forward to spending all of Eternity with all of you in our true Home – Paradise in Heaven.

To by beloved:

I love you from the breadth and depth that my soul can reach. Thank you, my beloved, for tending to my soul.

About the Author

Ryan Young is a Physician Assistant who lives and works in New York State. His wife, Elizabeth, is also a Physician Assistant. Ryan is a Knight of Malta and is in the Knights of Columbus. Ryan serves in a voluntary capacity as the Director of Camp Veritas, a Catholic camp for youth, and as Director of Fearless Ministries, Inc., a youth retreat organization. Ryan and his family were honored as the Knights of Columbus International Family of the Year in 2018. You can find more information about Camp Veritas at www.campveritas.com or about Fearless Ministries at www.fearlessretreats.org. Ryan and Elizabeth have been blessed with eight children: Christopher, Trinity, Grace, Mary, Justice, Faith, Xavier, and Michaela…so far…